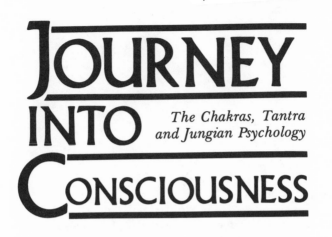

JOURNEY INTO CONSCIOUSNESS

The Chakras, Tantra and Jungian Psychology

CHARLES BREAUX

NICOLAS-HAYS, INC.
York Beach, Maine

First published in 1989 by
Nicolas-Hays, Inc.
Box 612
York Beach, ME 03910

Library of Congress Cataloging-in-Publication Data

Breaux, Charles.
    Journey into consciousness : the chakras, tantra, and Jungian psychology / by Charles Breaux.
        p.   cm.
    Bibliography: p.
    ISBN 0-89254-017-6
    1. Yoga (Tantric Buddhism)   2. Chakras.
3. Tantrism--Psychology.   4. Jung, C. G. (Carl Gustav),
1875-1961.   I. Title.
BQ7805.B74   1989
294.3'925--dc19   89-31263
                                                      CIP

Cover painting entitled *Ascending*
© 1980 Jeanette Stobie
Used by permission of Lightstream Paintings,
PO Box 3574, Redwood City, CA 94062

Typeset in 11 point Caslon
Printed in the United States of America by
Edwards Brothers, Inc.

JOURNEY

INTO

The Chakras, Tantra and Jungian Psychology

CONSCIOUSNESS

CONTENTS

Dedicated

to Gyalwa Karmapa, who made Buddhahood an unforgettable living reality for me;

to Landrian O'Donnel, dakini incarnate, who taught me the painful lesson of the price of my pride;

to Nanna Bolling, Barbara Hess, Inge Miller, and Dana and Tony Pasquale, for their love, support and assistance.

Special thanks to Sergei Diakoff and Äge Delbanco for their generosity.

◇

Introduction

When I was a teenager I bought my first book on yoga. In it was a picture of a meditating yogi with seven lotuses along his spine. The author mentioned a mysterious force (Kundalini) that rose up through the lotuses (chakras), and told of animals and strange deities that supposedly dwelled in these various chakras. These exotic images intrigued me, seeming to evoke ancient memories that I couldn't quite recall. My rational mind was left puzzling over the meaning of this strange Eastern "yoga." In college I began to read Theosophical literature. Leadbeater's book on the chakras, though very interesting, still left me confused as to how knowledge of the chakras could be useful to me.

Many years have passed and information about the chakras is commonplace in New Age circles, but no less confusing. Various authors and teachers, though convincingly dogmatic, are at odds as to the meaning and functions of the chakras. For instance, there are many discrepancies between the combinations of organs, endocrine glands, musical notes, colors and meanings attributed to the chakras, not to mention numerous cure-all techniques for balancing and clearing the chakras.

In this book I want to help lay a foundation for a practical psychological understanding of the chakras. Toward this end I will elaborate on the historical and philosophical context of Tantra, the native ground of the chakra system, and demonstrate how complementary it and Jungian psychology are. To begin, I would like to briefly share some of my experiences and background.

After graduating from college, where I studied psychology, philosophy, and world religions, my youthful idealism convinced me to pursue enlightenment–the only worthwhile goal. I became a modern-day recluse. A three-year period of seclusion and intense meditation resulted in an experience of the awakening of kundalini. For several days and nights a flaming pain burned in my pelvis and lower abdomen. Finally it moved up my spine and out the top of my head leaving me in a state of rapture for several weeks. I had expected to be transformed into some magical "enlightened" being, instead I found myself only at the beginning of an incredible journey.

This first encounter with kundalini stimulated the opening of clairvoyant and healing abilities. A year or so later, severe digestive problems, incurable with medical help, forced me to employ these abilities in order to heal myself. I then began working with others, and later taught classes in psychic awareness and healing. During this time I did a lot of experimenting with methods for working with the chakras. My background in psychology helped me to organize and interpret the psychic impressions I was seeing in the aura and chakras. I found Jungian psychology especially pertinent.

One auspicious day, a friend introduced me to Tibetan Tantra and I was allowed to attend a small private ceremony for the advanced students of Gyalwa Karmapa, the 16th incarnation of the head of the Kagyu lineage of Tibetan Buddhism. In this ceremony Karmapa placed a black crown on his head and transmitted a powerful spiritual force. I had a very profound experience and was inspired to follow Karmapa around the West Coast receiving instructions and initiations. In the years that followed, I studied at the feet of several other lamas and attended various meditation retreats. As I learned more about Tantra, I realized that many of the methods that I had intuitively developed to work with the chakras were very similar to Tantra.

In the spring of '81 I was once again embraced by the goddess Kundalini. Over a period of several months I had numerous encounters with her and experienced a series of Tantric initiations while in meditation. I also relived several lifetimes as a yogi and as a lama, giving me more insight into Tantra and why I was so fascinated by it.

Essentially, Tantra is concerned with our relationship to the primordial nature of the cosmos. How is it crystallized, or otherwise obscured, in the body-mind-soul? How are we transformed when it is released from its entrapment by the tendency to form an individual sense of identity? Are we and it the same thing? How do we find the answers to these questions? Gautama Buddha tied six knots in a silk handkerchief and asked a disciple how they could be undone. By tying the six knots, Buddha was showing how our individual identities are bound together by the knots of the ego self in each of the lower six chakras. He taught that we must untie them in the reverse order from which they were tied.

There is a commonly held belief that the awakening of Kundalini, occurring as the knots are loosened, is synonymous with reaching enlightenment. I must say it is not so easy. In fact, if we are not diligent in integrating the increased emergence of unconscious contents and karmic patterns, we may very well be cast mercilessly into a real live nightmare.

Carl Jung, in *Aspects of the Feminine*, indeed advises us to let sleeping dogs lie because the perilous journey into the unconscious is neither useful or necessary until we are driven to it out of necessity. He says that the fear of our inner side is sometimes a healthy one, because once we enter into its mysteries the scientific and moral standards of our "known" world erode from beneath our feet. He goes on to show how deeply set this fear of the inner world is by suggesting that it caused the primitive mind to create religious ideas and practices, and to empower the shaman and priest to protect us from it.[1]

Although the ancient system of Tantra stems from the same historical depths of the psyche, its conclusions and practices are unique. Tantra's relationship to our inner world—and life in general—is the main theme of this book; for now, I'll just point out that Tantra realizes that the vital forces of the cosmos are not different from those of the body-mind. A total acceptance of both, and the transformation of our awareness that results, are its primary concern.

This orientation is readily paralleled with Jungian psychology. From the Jungian perspective, we are involved in an ongoing process of realization called individuation. Through this process we, as individual units of life-consciousness, gradually expand our field of reference to embrace the personal and universal realms of the unconscious.

Individuation occurs through the experiences in our dream worlds and the events of our everyday lives; in fact, the outer world is considered by Jungians to be a blank screen onto which the images of the unconscious are projected. As in the Tantric view, our lives are seen as waking dreams, the spontaneous acting out of archetypal themes—ageless myths.

Life is living through us; acceptance of it, as it is, from its banality to its sublimeness, is the basis for our psychological as well as our spiritual growth. Hence in both Tantra and Jungian psychology, spiritual practices and therapeutic methods are vitally associated with a mindful participation in ordinary life.

Both Tantra and Jungian psychology appreciate the stages of the alchemical transformation of human consciousness. Tantra symbolizes our metamorphosis in a system of chakras that open as we awaken progressively to the various dimensions of the

---

[1]Carl Jung, *Aspects of the Feminine*, Bollingen Series (Princeton, NJ: Princeton University Press, 1982), p. 92.

psyche. In each of these seven chakras, deities and other symbols portray the contents and their functions found at each level. From the Jungian perspective, universal themes present in the myriad stories of heroes and heroines, and gods and goddesses, evident throughout the world, are dramatizations of the developmental stages of our growth in consciousness.

In *The Origins and History of Consciousness*, Jungian analyst Erich Neumann shows how we, as individuals, pass through the same stages of development that humankind has collectively evolved through. Projected into the world's mythology, these archetypal phases start and end with images of the Tail-Eating Serpent (Uroboros). The in-between stages include: the World Creation, the Great Mother, Separation of the World Parents, the Birth and Trials of the Hero, the Slaying of the Dragon, the Rescue and Romance with the Captive Maiden, and the Transformation and Deification of the Hero. In the text that follows, I will be relating these archetypal stages to the seven chakras.

There are many ways that Tantric practices and Jungian Psychology coincide and enhance each other. Western psychology owes a tremendous appreciation for, and indeed apprenticeship to, the many thousands of years of Tantric research into the transpersonal realms of the psyche. Tantra, in return, benefits from the practical knowledge about dealing with the more contemporary and personal aspects of Western psychological processes.

In Hindu and Buddhist Tantra, there are many different sects and a cornucopia of teachings. I have drawn mostly from Tibetan Tantra because of my firsthand experience of it and because it is still very much alive in our era. I distilled from it what I feel is most fundamental, and present this essence, when possible, through the medium of Jungian psychology.

The language of Tantra is visionary; rich in symbols and metaphors produced spontaneously in the meditations of ancient yogis. It is best in some cases to allow these to communicate to your deeper self instead of attempting a translation for the rational mind, hence I have included a meditation practice at the end of each chapter employing Tibetan Tantric Deities and procedures. This is the best way to convey what Tantra actually is.

Although drawn directly from firsthand experience, I want to make it clear to the reader that what I present is not to be mistaken for orthodox Tibetan Buddhism. I am presenting a way that the Tantric method can be integrated with contemporary Western approaches to the healing and development of the body-mind. In conveying the fundamental outlook of Tibetan Tantra, I have stripped much of its cultural trappings. Jamgon Kongtrul, in *The Torch of Certainty*, explains how our Western minds have difficulty fully grasping the cultural background of the Tibetan tradition. He concludes that it is inappropriate and unnecessary to impose it on us. Presenting the "basic mind works" of the teachings is all that is required.[2]

At first glance, Tantric doctrine could be judged as a bizarre mythology or superstition by those of us steeped in Western rationalism. There are few who are not students of Jungian psychology or students of mythology who can appreciate the psychological truths beautifully woven into the fabric of the Tantric teachings. For the average person, therefore, the essential teachings are best explained in terms that are easy to grasp and accept. There is a need for a synthesis, a meeting ground, between the Tantric approach and our Western scientific viewpoint.

Fortunately this meeting ground is fairly well established; scientific evidence of parapsychological events is now considerable. Telepathy, clairvoyance, reincarnation, auras, and even the existence and emanations of the chakras have all been scientifically investigated and to some extent verified.[3] The similarities

---

[2]Jamgon Kongrul, *The Torch of Certainty* (Boston: Shambhala, 1986), pp. 12–13.
[3]A commendable reference is *Hands of Light*, by Barbara Ann Brennan (NY: Bantam, 1987).

between the world views of the mystic and the modern physicist have also been explored. It is in this middle ground that I bring together the two systems of Tibetan Tantra and Jungian psychology.

The next issue that I had to face in presenting Tantric teachings was personal: I have taken vows not to reveal many of the teachings I received. I have worked around this by not discussing any methods here that have not been published elsewhere, and by sharing insights from my personal experiences with the methods.

It is unquestionable that the Tantric methods offered in this book will be more effective when empowered by a lama within the proper context. Nonetheless, due to their archetypal significance, I feel the visualizations presented in the earlier chapters can be useful to any serious practitioner. However, the more advanced techniques briefly outlined in chapters 6 through 8, should not be experimented with without the guidance of a competent teacher.

A Jungian therapist and a Tibetan lama perform a similar service for their respective clients and students. Both are veterans of the inner journey who guide us through the perils and pitfalls, if we cooperate, on our quest for healing and wholeness. There are many valuable psychological self-help books, but we cannot compare their assistance to a skilled therapist. Likewise, this book is no substitute for a genuine Tantric teacher. If you are attracted to the Tibetan teachings and practices, I strongly encourage you to seek out one of the many Dharma centers in the Western world.

The practices in the Tibetan Tradition were written by men and primarily intended to be used by men. In the meditations that I present here, there has been some attempt to balance the male and female perspectives. Some of the visualizations and procedures presented here have therefore been altered to accommodate women. Nonetheless, in some meditations, a man will be required to identify with a female deity; in other instances, a woman will have to visualize herself as a male deity.

There are numerous minor discrepancies between different sects and traditions regarding deities and meditation practices; we are not dealing with a precise scientific "hard" reality here, but the vital chameleon nature of the psyche. I have, therefore, tried to demonstrate the essential principles of the Tantric method. If you choose to experiment with the methods that I describe, please consider them as symbols or tools that can guide you to your own inner experiences. Allow them to become living realities through the archetypal forces, and the teacher within yourself (the Buddha-Mind, or in Jungian terms, the Self) that they are capable of evoking.

Now, in conclusion, I have an axe to grind. A young woman who had been living at the ashram of a well-known "mass market guru" came to me suffering from severe lower back pain and infla-mation of her female organs. She had been strictly celibate while engaging in numerous hours of Kundalini Yoga on a daily basis as per the instructions of her mentor. I tried to diplomatically point out that perhaps her physical problems were related to festering emotional issues. When I suggested therapeutic methods to help her integrate some of these issues, she became very defensive and confided that she didn't need to deal with that stuff because her spiritual practice and her teacher would take care of it.

I had a very difficult time believing that her teacher was encouraging her to continue to activate the Kundalini while she was desperately repressing it from flowing up through her second and third chakras, because she "didn't want to deal with that stuff." But about six months later, right there in the ashram, the dam broke and she was committed to a psychiatric ward.

Over the years I have witnessed similar examples of people who, through sheer willpower and religious idealism, ignore their psychological responsibilities while questing after some spiritual panacea. Many of these well-meaning "spiritual schizophrenics" were being courted by the now commonplace charismatic and often self-proclaimed guru.

Spiritual unfoldment occurs only through the unimpeded flow of the primordial power of the cosmos through the body-mind. This may happen gradually or in dramatic spurts, depending on such variables as the degree of opening that has taken place in previous lifetimes and the amount of psychological resistance in the present life. I personally believe that it is wiser and safer to work at removing psychological blocks (which means you first have to recognize that they are there and be willing to work them out) than it is to use techniques to force kundalini to awaken.

Enlightenment is a fruition of psychological maturity, and your ability to grow and develop psychologically cannot be isolated from the fullfilment of your physical needs. These three aspects of yourself are not separate from one another, they are part of a continuum. This is not necessarily a new idea, but a very important one.

In other words, the ego-self is your vehicle through which you grow. Gautama Buddha used this metaphor: the ego-self is like a raft that carries you across the river of life. Without it you cannot cross, but once you reach the yonder shore it is no longer needed, in fact it would be quite cumbersome to attempt to drag it behind you as you go on to climb the lofty peaks of consciousness.

The format of this book begins in the root chakra and follows the path of your physical-psychological-spiritual continuum up through the chakras, seen in this perspective as progressive stages in the evolution of the psyche. This path doesn't always hug the ridge tops; it often falls into deep canyons, sometimes moves along the waterways, across the valleys, deserts, and the tall peaks of your inner self. Its direction may not always seem clear as you venture into the wilderness within.

When you step out of your own shadow, you enter the light within. It is then you realize that beneath all your fears, desires, pains, and preconceptions of the ego-self surges the basic drive to remember your essential nature. This is the same ongoing process, no matter what you might call it. Though approaching this process from opposite ends of the historical spectrum, and from opposite sides of the earth, both Tantra and Jungian psychology aspire to fathom this mysterious process and create the necessary conditions in the body-mind so that this spiritual transformation can occur.

CHAPTER
ONE

◆

TANTRIC
ROOTS AND
RELEVANCE

*N*o one knows how old Tantra is. The earliest published texts are Hindu, dated 500 A.D. The first Buddhist text appeared about 600 A.D., but there are earlier unpublished teachings that were transmitted directly from teacher to student for many hundreds of years. The roots of Tantra, however, are embedded in the early history of Indian culture. Hindu and Buddhist Tantra are the main trunks of a tree that grew out of ancient cults and oral traditions, which branched out to Nepal, Tibet, Mongolia, China, Japan, Cambodia, Java, the Near East, and, more recently, the Western world.

The undisturbed civilization of ancient India allowed Tantra to unfold from the fertile depths of the mythological mind and blossom through some of the world's most devoted spiritual thinkers. Some of its myth and ritual may be as old as the Paleolithic period (c. 20,000 B.C.). In the prehistoric cave complex of Pech-Merle in France, for instance, there is a chamber with female emblems which, Philip Rawson points out, are very similar to those still worshipped today in Indian shrines.[1]

In prehistorical cultures the creative power of the cosmos was generally worshipped as the Mother Goddess; the early Indus culture was no exception. Represented in various Indus artifacts, she is often associated with animals, whose sacred and cultic values were related to their strength and sexual virility.

The emphasis on fertility was not confined to goddess and animal images. There were the male figures seated in yogic postures wearing horned headdresses and brandishing erect penises. Erect phalluses carved from stone, some as large as two feet high, also displayed this early worship of the generative powers of nature.

The god Shiva, who eventually became a major deity in Hindu Tantra, was obviously a development of these Indus cults. Shiva is often depicted like the horned god of the Indus seals, seated in yogic posture with an erect penis. His universal symbol is an erect phallus (lingam), and his vehicle is Nandi the bull.

In ancient India, the only major social upheaval was the invasion of Indo-Europeans (the Aryans) around 1500 B.C. The Aryans brought with them a pantheon of sky gods, a group of priests that recited hymns and performed rituals, and a psychoactive substance called soma which induced states of ecstasy and proffered magical powers. The Aryans were a warlike and patriarchal culture. Through their rituals and magic powers, they believed they controlled the gods. Their rituals grew in time into complex simulations for the entire cosmos, and the priesthood became a powerful hierarchy.

Worship of local goddesses, stemming from the earliest Indus cults, continued to flourish independent of this Vedic tradition. Many popular cults formed around different goddesses and

---

[1]Philip Rawson, *Tantra: The Indian Cult of Ecstasy* (New York: Avon, 1973), p. 7.

modes of worship. As all animal life comes from the womb of the female, the universe was mythically seen to proceed from the Goddess. It is She who embodies consciousness in the world of matter and the senses and, in turn, liberates it. A woman within whom the Goddess was realized was, therefore, highly revered and ritual intercourse with her was considered an initiation into the mysteries.

These cult practices were very contrary to orthodox Vedic traditions. Whereas in Tantra sexual energy was worshipped and enjoyed as a way of being joined to cosmic processes, the Vedic traditions favored a repressive hoarding of the sacred sexual power. Ascetic disciplines were related to social position; for the priest or ruling class person, the storing up of this sacred power was very important because it supposedly filled his body with spiritual energy, magical powers were thereby supposedly acquired.

Around the fifth century B.C., there were many political and economic changes in the Aryan culture. Popular religious practices, long oppressed by the Vedic tradition, emerged and combined with new systems of thought. These systems stressed personal effort rather than dogma, and were based on the experience of teachers who exemplified the fruits of their spiritual practices. Hence, great teachers like Mahavira, the founder of the Jain movement, and Gautama Siddhartha, founder of Buddhism, attracted many earnest seekers.

In the centuries that followed, the Vedic tradition imitated many of the meditation methods, deities, and philosophical elements of these popular religions. What is known as yoga today is a result of this synthesis.

The yogic system was a discipline by which the body, mind, and senses could be yoked to the spiritual nature. A superconscious state was thereby attained, causing the distinction between the self and the Self (experienced as pure universal consciousness) to dissolve.

In the yogic system popular personal deities replaced the supreme impersonal Vedic god Brahman, who represented the Absolute beyond name and form. Shiva and Vishnu, for example, became personalized gods and centers of focus for yogic systems that incorporated ancient Tantric practices. These yogas became the vehicle for what we shall refer to as Hindu Tantra.

Buddhism was a another significant product of the religious renaissance during this time in India. Siddhartha Gautama, a young prince later to be renowned as the Buddha, forsook his family and royal heritage to pursue a spiritual life. He traveled through India studying with different teachers and sects, eventually rejecting their austere methods and hair-splitting metaphysics to found the Middle Way. His down to earth, heart of the matter teachings were canonized into the Hinayana (lesser vehicle) school of Buddhism by his surviving students. About 500 years later, a greatly expanded doctrine became known as the Mahayana (greater vehicle) school of Buddhism. During the next several hundred years, more and more Tantric elements were integrated into Buddhism.

Buddhist Tantra evolved either secretly and/or slowly for nearly a millennium, blossoming in its full glory between the eighth and twelfth centuries. In juxtaposition to the great orthodox Buddhist universities, Buddhist Tantra was propagated by eccentric sages, the more famous of whom were long-haired itinerants, who scoffed the rigid monastic traditions and the narrowminded conventions of the Hindu caste system to practice the "Crazy Wisdom." These Mahasiddhas—yogis with great (*maha*) powers (*siddhas*)—enjoyed their mystical experiences while amusing themselves in the sport of mundane reality. They taught by example rather than by the intellect. The existential freedom of their lives often gave way to behaviors and events that shattered the rigid structures of students' minds with potent and bizarre metaphors.

During the time of the Mahasiddhas, India was being assailed by Islamic armies. By the 12th century, Buddhism had been uprooted from the Indian soil by militant Muslims. Tantric Buddhism by that time had been successfully transplanted to Tibet.

When Tantric Buddhism was brought to Tibet, it confronted the native Bön religion, an ancient shamanic tradition. There are vivid stories that tell how powerful yogis tamed the terrifying demons of the old Bön religion with their magic powers. Once tamed, these demons became guardians of the Buddhist teachings and were incorporated into the Buddhist pantheon of meditation deities.

Hindu Tantra survives in myriad popular and obscure cults, but was never canonized into a definite institution. The Tibetan tradition, on the other hand, developed its own form of theocracy and established an institution similar to the Catholic Church. Traced back to 749 A.D., when the Indian Sage Padma Sambhava brought the Buddhist Tantras to Tibet, the teachings have been preserved and enhanced by a lineage of enlightened lamas who return lifetime after lifetime. Specially trained clairvoyant lamas locate these reincarnated teachers and bring them to monasteries at a very early age. Often these special lamas will leave a letter giving the exact time and place of their next incarnation. This is one example of the precision of the Tibetan techniques and evidence that their power has been vitally maintained.

Buddhist Tantra has recently come to the West and is quickly rooting itself in the minds of earnest seekers. This was in fact prophesied by the great yogi Padma Sambhava who said that Buddhist teachings would come to the land of the Red Man when the Tibetan people would be scattered like ants, the iron bird flies, and horses run on wheels. Because of the Communist invasion of Tibet, this eighth century prophecy of Padma Sambhava is becoming a reality. The main centers of Tibetan Buddhism are now in such places as the Naropa Institute in Colorado, and the Nyingma Institute in California. Tibetan Tantra is mingling with our Western approaches to the development and healing of the human psyche. Both disciplines are being altered and enriched by this exchange.

The word tantra is derived from the Sanskrit root *tan*; meaning "to continue, multiply, expand on." In ancient India it was used as the verb "to weave." Yogis borrowed it to describe the interwoven nature of the world and our actions, the continuity of cause and effect, and the essential interdependence of everything that exists. The teachings and texts that became known as Tantra are based on a mystical experience that braids the practitioner's mind into the seamless fabric of Absolute Reality.

At the heart of Tantra is the experience of a divine power within the human being that can be awakened. The physical body is considered to be the locus for this power, and hence the focus of ritual practice. This inner power was named Kundalini by the ancient yogis. It is possible that its active role in the development of Tantra may stem back to prehistoric times, for an example of a very similar practice has been found in a primitive tribe in Africa. In a documentary film by a Harvard research team, the ceremonial dance of the !Kung shows bushmen dancing for hours to heat up a psychic power called n\um. The n\um rises up from the base of the spine to the skull producing a trance state. The !Kung believe that n\um is a supernatural power that heals them.

The human organism in Tantra is experienced as a microcosm of the cosmos. Tantric practitioners are concerned with transforming consciousness so they can realize the illusionary nature of their normal sense of identity and experience directly their essential unity with the macrocosm.

Within the body-mind there are major centers of psychic energy called chakras, where specific deities, with their unique psychological and spiritual forces, reside. These centers, and their respective deities, form the basis for a complex system of myth and ritual in Tantra.

In addition to the central role of the chakra system and the evocation of the primordial power of creation in meditation rituals, Tantra is characterized in several other significant ways. Most definitive is the visualization of various deities. A practitioner learns to chant the sacred mantras, mimic the body postures, and identify with various deities in meditation while experiencing their supernal state of awareness.

Another important difference between Tantra and most spiritual traditions is its non-theistic experience of Absolute Reality. Though Tantra uses gods and goddesses to symbolize various spiritual forces and higher states of consciousness, the cosmos is viewed as a spontaneous act of ongoing creation arising out of a womb-like emptiness pregnant with unlimited potential. This great emptiness is associated with pure consciousness and its spatial quality is the unchanging ground out of which all phenomena emerge. Whereas most religions conceive of a supreme being, "God," who creates, governs, and is therefore separate from the universe, Absolute Reality in Tantra is realized in meditation as an intrinsic state of Being-Consciousness.

Most spiritual paths turn away from the mundane in an attempt to transcend the world. Dualistic values like light and dark, spiritual and material, good and evil, are at their foundations. Tantra sees the same cosmic forces that create the world as existing within us; there is no separation, no good and evil. The forces that crystallize into the material world are none other than sublime cosmic forces, which can be converted back into their pristine state. Tantra, therefore, embraces all that is human within us. The energy of sex, of emotion, of thought, and all action is transmuted through skillful means into their generic essence.

Tantra has, therefore, often been considered a left hand path (taboo and dangerous) due to its unconventionality. But for thousands of years Tantra has explored the many dimensions of the human psyche. Out of its solid foundation of sympathetic magic, mythology and the ritual sublimation of human sexuality, Tantra intuited a holistic psychology which encompassed such fields of endeavor as astronomy-astrology, medicine, mathematics, and alchemy-chemistry. Though couched in a mythological language, Tantra's insights into the nature of the cosmos have indeed a striking resemblance to modern physics.

Throughout its long history, Tantra has suffered much opposition and exile at the hands of orthodox society. But its spirit has vitally survived and readily adapted itself to new environments. Tantra has created this animosity by confronting the basic schizoid tendencies of social and religious traditions in an attempt to liberate its followers from the collective neurosis that conventional traditions breed.

Tantra, above all, is a path of action. More than a rigid set of rationalizations about spiritual matters, it is a collection of methods that can lead us to a state of inner realization. It is a way of being in the process of self-actualization. Its goal is simply to be. The path is never ending. At higher levels of attainment Tantra is a spontaneous way of being fully conscious while abiding calmly in the womb of creation.

Tantra is not limited to any "ism" or sect, nor is it necessarily a religion. As an empirical and experiential set of methods, Tantra is as valid and timely today as in any period of its long history.

◇

Hindu Tantra

Having constructed a philosophical and historical backdrop, let's look more closely at the basic principles and elements of Tantra. Hindu Tantra is composed of the metaphors and symbols that were inherited directly from ancient cults. We will therefore begin with this before going on to study how these metaphors and symbols were integrated into Buddhism.

Absolute Reality (pristine consciousness) is personified in one form of Hindu Tantra as Shiva. Ancient yogis imagined the body of the cosmos to be Shiva's lover. She has many names to express her various forms, but is generally known as Shakti. When giving form to the formless and limiting the infinite, she is called Maya Shakti. The word *maya* comes from the Sanskrit root *ma*, which means to measure, to form, to exhibit. Through her divine imagination, Maya Shakti conjures up the great illusion of the universe by veiling pure consciousness in many layers of matter. This apparition (maya) does not mean that the world does not exist; but its true nature is hidden because of our obscured minds. (See fig. 1 on page 10.)

Shakti is also worshipped as the revealer of the truth and the Great Liberator. All she brings into temporal existence will some-day return to its original essence. This function of the goddess is personified as the awe-inspiring Kali. To the ego-centered person attached to the material world, she is a wrathful and horrifying goddess of destruction. To a yogi in search of liberation from the illusion and suffering of the ego identity, she is a saviouress.

The sexual imagery of Shiva and Shakti as lovers points towards their interdependence. Although apparently separate, they are in truth two complementary aspects of a single unity; one cannot exist without the other. This double-sexed supreme deity is thus both temporal and infinite. Shiva is the unlimited whole, Shakti is the ongoing convergence of parts that forever make up the whole; Shiva is transcendent and changeless, and Shakti is phenomenal and mutable.

In *Tantra, the Indian Cult of Ecstasy*, Philip Rawson describes the Tantric view of the cosmos as an interwoven web of vibrations, or subtle resonances. Originating in the most rarified "substance" of creation, these vibrational patterns overlap and intermingle until they appear to solidify. The generic sound-substance

Figure 1. Mahamaya: the Supreme Shakti emerging from the Shiva lingam. From *Icons of Buddhist and Brahmanical Sculptures in the Dacca Museum*, by Nalini Kunta Bhattasali, M. A. Published by Rai S. N. Bhadra Bahadus, Dacca Museum Committee, 1929.

comes from Shakti's tinkling anklet as she dances. As the rhythms of her dance increase in complexity and passion, the fabric of the universe is woven into seven major layers of density.[2] The seven chakras (major energy centers along the spine) of the human microcosm are correlated to this seven-fold division of the macrocosm.

The seventh chakra, at the top of the head, is related to the original union of Shiva and Shakti. In the sixth chakra, in the center of the head, Shakti has separated from Shiva and created the realm of the mind (*manas*). The five remaining chakras, located from the neck to the pelvis, represent progressive crystal-lizations, symbolized by the five elements: ether, air, fire, water, and earth. Each stage is denser, as it contracts out of the previous element, until the solidity of the earth element is formed. (See fig. 2 on page 12.)

After Shakti has created the world, she is imagined to hibernate in the depths of the material universe. According to Joseph Campbell, the Sanskrit word *kundalin* means "that which is coiled or spiral in nature" and refers to the spiral patterns of energy found throughout the natural world, from the DNA molecule to the shape of galaxies. When the long terminal *I* is added, it becomes *kundalini*, a feminine noun meaning "snake."[3] A serpent rests in a coil and, like a spring, can release its potential energy when it strikes. Tantra's mythological mind compiled all these factors into the personification of Kundalini Shakti, the slumbering primordial power in nature. In the hologram of the body-mind it rests in the earth element, in the first chakra at the floor of the pelvis.

The involutionary flow of Kundalini coming into the seventh chakra divides into three channels in the sixth chakra. See fig. 3.

---

[2]Rawson, *Tantra*, p. 196.
[3]Joseph Campbell, *The Mythic Image* (Princeton, NJ: Princeton University Press, 1974), p. 331.

7
SAHASRARA-PADMA
Crown center
Seed-syllable: OM

In the Tibetan system conceived as One Center *hdab-stori*

6
AJNA-CHAKRA
Between the eyebrows
Seed-syllable: half or short A

5
VISUDDHA-CHAKRA
Throat center
Element: Ether, as substrate of sound (*sabda*)
Seed syllable: HAM
Color: white
Form: circle

4
ANAHATA-CHAKRA
Heart center
Element: Air (motion)
Seed-syllable: YAM
Color: gray-blue
Form: interlaced triangles

3
MANIPURA-CHAKRA
Solar plexus
Element: fire
Seed-syllable: RAM
Color: red
Form: inverted triangle

2
SVADHISTHANA-CHAKRA
Abdominal center (4 finger-widths below the navel)
Element: water
Seed-syllable: VAM
Color: white
Form: crescent

In the Tibetan system combined under the name Sang-Na (*gsang-gnas*)

1
MULADHARA-CHAKRA
Root center (in the perineum). Its latent primordial force is represented by the serpent, Kundalini, coiled around the Lingam in the center of the triangular Yoni.
Element: earth
Seed-syllable: LAM
Color: yellow
Form: square

Figure 2. Hindu chakras. In Tibetan Tantra, the first and second chakras are combined, and the sixth and seventh chakras are combined. Illustration from *Foundations of Tibetan Mysticism*, by Lama Govinda, published by Samuel Weiser, York Beach, ME and Rider & Co., London, reproduced by permission of the publishers.

In the normal person, Kundalini flows down the left and right channels, supplying all the sense organs and faculties of awareness that maintain the illusion of the world. While Kundalini rests in this state, our lives are dominated by the blind forces of the instincts, desires, and concepts of the ego-self. This divine energy can be withdrawn from these mechanisms of the body-mind and directed back up the central channel. When this occurs, the Serpent Goddess awakens. Rising up through the psyche, she unveils herself in each of the chakras to reveal higher and higher levels of consciousness. Ultimately our awareness is released from the limitations of embodiment and partakes in the divine pleasure of Shiva and Shakti's lovemaking. This is the Great Bliss and Wisdom which Tantra says is the ground of being and the highest goal to be attained.

The language and imagery of sexual union are used here to indicate the mystical ecstasy that the ancient yogis experienced as

Figure 3. Ida, Pingala, and Sushumna. The Ida and Pingala are secondary involutionary energies spiralling down the central primary evolutionary channel, Sushumna. In Buddhist Tantra, the Ida and Pingala are visualized running parallel to the central channel. All three channels converge in the first chakra where Kundalini lies dormant until awakened.

a result of their practices. In the mythological minds of these yogis, the sexual energy of the microcosm directly linked them with the creative powers of the macrocosm. Sexual energy was sacred and enjoyed in a ritual called the Chakrapuja. This ritual was performed in a circle, the teacher and his or her consort sat in the center. Participating couples enjoyed five substances, representing the five elements. These consist of wine, meat, fish, an aphrodisiac made from parched grains, and sexual intercourse.

Through this disciplined ritual, participants transmuted inclinations of passion and sensual gratification by learning to see the Goddess in all things. Sexual intercourse was used to arouse Kundalini while couples identified themselves with Shakti and Shiva. There were variations on this ritual in which a single yogi would unite with a symbolic number of consorts to act out various cosmic events. These ancient rituals served as the inspiration for complex internal meditations and the symbolic sexual iconography of later Tantric systems.

Another Hindu practice, Kundalini yoga, involved a rich mythological assortment of symbols, animals, and a mixture of pre-Aryan and Vedic deities that were visualized in the various chakras during meditational rituals. The movement of the Goddess Kundalini supposedly varies as it progresses through the different chakras. In the Hindu diagrams of the chakras, different animals symbolize these movements and are considered the vehicle of the primary deity in each chakra.

The Kundalini energy also assumes a specific frequency pattern at each chakra level. These are depicted in the Indian symbology by the seed (bija) mantras in the center of each lotus diagram. The number of petals of each chakra also refers literally to its vibrational frequency. The lowest chakra, for example, has four petals which represent the low vibration of the material world. On the other end of the spectrum, the crown chakra has one thousand petals which symbolize the high vibrational rate of transcendent realms.

Kundalini yoga begins in the first chakra, stimulating the dormant Kundalini by visualizing the lotus of the first chakra on the floor of the pelvis. The seed mantra (*LAM*) is imagined in the center of this lotus as it is recited, either silently or aloud. From the radiant form of the seed mantra all the symbolic elements contained within the lotus emerge in sequential order. Each deity and symbol is then contemplated and then drawn back into the seed mantra. The seed mantra itself is then imagined to rise up into the lotus of the second chakra where it is absorbed into the seed mantra there.

The second chakra is visualized below the navel. As the seed mantra in its center is intoned, all of the elements of the second chakra emerge and are meditated on. When this is completed, these contents are drawn back into the seed mantra, which in turn ascends to the third chakra in the solar plexus.

This procedure repeats itself up to the seventh chakra, whereupon the yogi's awareness enters the sky-like emptiness of pure consciousness. Like a flame burning in a windless place, the meditator endeavors to focus his or her awareness in this state.

The meditation ritual is completed by recreating the body-mind. Starting in the seventh chakra and descending through the body, each chakra is visualized precipitating from the next higher one.

The knowledge and practice of Kundalini Yoga has been passed down from teacher to disciple since antiquity. Although this transmission occurred in part through various forms of ritualized sex in the mainstream of ancient Hindu Tantric practices, it was also passed on through a practice called Shaktipat. A person who has awakened this cosmic power can transmit it to another in various ways: by touch, by thought transference, sacred chants, or by merely looking into the eyes of the student. Aside from their expert advice and the imparting of methods and knowledge, a teacher is important on the Tantric path because he or she has this ability to stimulate and safely guide the awakening of the Kundalini force.

When Kundalini is activated, its increased flow stirs unconscious contents, which then can flood into awareness. To resist any of these occurrences can be dangerous, as the power may become trapped or its circulation distorted in the channels of the subtle bodies. Severe physical or psychological imbalances could then occur.

To help prepare the yogi for these intense encounters with the unconscious, there were different levels, or types, of yoga. Hatha Yoga strengthened and purified the physical body. Bakti Yoga harmonized the emotional nature with devotion and spiritual desires. Raja Yoga trained the mind and nourished it with philosophical truths. These all led to Mahayoga, sometimes referred to as Siddhayoga, which was concerned with awakening Kundalini. Many years of arduous training traditionally took place with a teacher, who embodied the awakened power of Kundalini.

◇

Buddist Tantra

There is a great deal of controversy between Buddhists and Hindus regarding the origin of Tantra. Some scholars maintain that Buddhist Tantra evolved out of Hindu Tantra, and even later reverted to it. Buddhists naturally believe that Gautama Buddha was the originator of their Tantra, which could very well be true in the sense that he spent considerable time wandering through the holy lands of India sampling various teachers and methods. Early Buddhist scriptures indicate that Gautama was at least acquainted with the knowledge of the chakras and inner fire. It is quite possible that he was instructed in the ancient Tantric arts and then later revised or reinterpreted them.

It is also possible that some of the more elaborate Buddhist Tantric meditation methods weren't introduced into the Buddhist canon until several centuries after his death. With the advent of Mahayana Buddhism, a more liberal and expanded form of Buddhism, the word Buddha referred more to the potential of the Enlightened-Mind inherent within all of us, than it did to Gautama the Buddha. In this sense, various "awakened" (Buddha means one who has awakened) Buddhist yogis may have integrated Tantric elements, or spontaneously created certain meditation procedures, which became part of the Buddhist Tantric doctrine. Buddha, *i.e.*, the Enlightened-Mind, would naturally have been considered the source of their inspiration.

In Buddhist Tantra, we find many of the symbols, deities, rituals, and meditation practices found in Hindu Tantra, but their meanings are often quite different. Buddhist Tantra also contains three principal aspects that they consider make it superior to Hindu Tantra: renunciation, enlightened attitude, and the right philosophy.

Renunciation, as used here, means giving up the belief in individual identity. Buddha realized that an individual was composed of five elements of grasping (*skandhas*): form, feelings, cognition (or rapport), mental fabrications with volition, and consciousness. What is called the self is only these five elements shaped by past events and desires. Unlike Hindu Tantra, which postulates an eternal self (Atman), Gautama Buddha realized that there is no independent or eternal self that exists apart from this bundle of aggregates. Our belief in such a self is the root cause of all our suffering according to the Buddhist.

The enlightened attitude refers to the Bodhisattva ideal, which changes the motivation to reach enlightenment from one of personal gain to one of compassion for all beings.

The right philosophy is based on the comprehension of the essential emptiness of reality. All phenomena are transient, void of absolute existence and dependent on other temporal phenomena. The origination of all phenomena from other transitory factors, and not from a single independent or absolute entity (such as God), was called dependent origination in Buddhism. Absolute Reality is the Void, the unchanging and undefinable no-thingness in which everything arises and passes away.

The continuing existence of any person (*i.e.*, bundle of aggregates) is the result of ignorance and desire. Ignorance of the impermanence of all existence leads to the desire for the continuance of individual identity. Desire welds the bundle of aggregates together and motivates us to gain satisfaction from what is inherently impermanent. Such attempts always lead to disappointment and to various forms of suffering. Liberation in Buddhism occurs when ignorance and attachment end. What we are freed from is the deluded perception of the world and the conviction that we exist as an independent ego-self.

Because the capacity of an ego-bound unit of consciousness is finite, it is virtually impossible to directly perceive the Void. Therefore Buddhist Tantra guides the student through a step-by-step unfoldment. The first step (Kriyatantra) emphasizes our actions, which are formalized into symbolic rituals. This first step also focuses on purification of the body-mind. The second step (Caryatantra) concentrates on understanding the implications of the activities of Kriyatantra. It seeks to balance external ritual actions with awareness cultivated in meditation. Yogatantra is a continuation of this development of insight, with emphasis on internal practices. This leads to the final step of Mahayogatantra. This Tantra stresses the importance of penetrative insight into the void nature of reality, a spontaneous mode of action, and a continuous state of meditational equipose that unites the two.

The Tibetan Book of the Dead (the Bardo Thodol) is one of the foundations for the Buddhist Tantric system. Under the guise of a death experience, it metaphorically outlines the dimensions of the psyche and the way of liberation. The cosmology of the *Tibetan Book of the Dead* is based on five primordial Buddhas. These five core Buddhas are correlated with the five cosmic elements (related to the skandhas or elements of grasping mentioned earlier), and consequently, with the five chakras of the Tibetan Buddhist map of the psychic body.

The five wisdom-energies radiate from the Void and subdivide to make possible all mental creations. When the process is reversed in meditation, their wisdom conquers the illusions of our mundane perception of the world. Hence they are also referred to as the conquerors, because they not only create the "appearance" of the world in our minds, but dispel it with their wisdom-energy.

In order to fit the scheme of the five primordial Buddhas, the Buddhists sometimes combine the functions of the first and second chakras and the sixth and seventh chakras, and in practice only the four higher chakras are normally used. Each of the five Buddhas represent one kind of deluded perception (related to a particular chakra), and its antidotal wisdom-energy.

Each of the five chakras in the Buddhist system are expressions of different aspects of the mind. Vital energy (*prana*) is related to both the breath and the mind. This means that any state of mind will have a corresponding type of prana, often reflected in the character of the breath. The mind and prana are therefore inseparable in action. Through meditation and breathing techniques, the prana of each chakra is stimulated. As a result, repressed emotions and various unconscious states of mind are brought into consciousness.

The goal of controlling the pranas is to eventually purge them of their mental-emotional aberrations by leading them into the central channel, where these vital airs will feed the inner fire. Removing the vital energy from the delusions of the ego, the mental-emotional element of each chakra is purified and transformed into its original wisdom-energy. As in the Hindu system,

Figure 4. Mahakala. An example of a wrathful deity who serves as a protector. Mahakala is a Buddhist version of the Hindu Deity Bhairava, a fierce form of Shiva. From the Thanka collection of Sergei Diakoff. Reproduced by permission.

this leads to the reversal of genesis, i.e., the five elemental states of "mind-matter" are progressively rarified.

Dumo (the Buddhist equivalent to kundalini) is a term denoting a ferocious woman who annihilates all desires and passions. Various visualizations and breathing exercises (sexual energy may also be used to aid in producing the inner fire, either with a skilled consort or through visualization) change the body-mind into an unobstructed channel for the Dumo fire. The yogi then becomes adept in directing the flow of this powerful force. Initiates demonstrate their mastery by passing specific tests. For instance, they may be required to meditate in the snow in wet clothing. If they are competent, they can actually dry their clothing and remain warm in the freezing cold![4]

The five primordial Buddhas, as the core emanations of the Void, are considered to be the progenitors of the five families of gods and goddesses which constitute the Buddhist pantheon. Thus, a variety of deities are shown in meditational diagrams (mandalas) used to indicate certain spiritual principles and their interactions at different stages of psychic integration. In some mandalas, the primordial Buddhas are depicted in union with female partners. This represents the five kinds of creative-energies interacting with their five complementary wisdom-energies. Other deities surround the central Buddhas in mandalas designed for specific initiations.

Wrathful deities illustrate the world of the five wisdoms clouded by the passions and delusions of sentient beings still under the sway of ignorance. The fierce expressions and clenched teeth of these deities demonstrate the power and strength needed to battle against the ego and its delusions. (See fig. 4 on page 20.) Their weapons are used for cutting through hindrances, and the corpses beneath their feet are the passions

---

[4] I will not accept responsibility for any reader, who, with no proper training, tries to do this.

they have slain. In advanced levels of Tibetan Tantra, the power of these wrathful deities is used to conquer the baser portions of the psyche and initiate one into the highest attainments of wisdom-energy.

The female in Buddhist Tantra is correlated with wisdom and called Prajna, rather than Shakti, as in Hindu Tantra. The male principle is related to skillful means. The god and goddess in sexual embrace, therefore, represent the union of wisdom-insight with skillful means.

The gods or goddesses in the Tibetan pantheon may be visualized in meditation as mentors and guardians. For example, for a man who is inspired or excited by the beauty of women, a lovely goddess is employed to transmute his romantic feelings. Such a goddess is called a dakini. The term dakini literally means "sky goer," or one who moves through the sky. Commonly appearing as a goddess, peaceful or wrathful, she is also experienced as the various forces (related to the five Buddha families) that are at play through all phenomena. The yogi begins by visualizing her in daily meditation. He may then join with her in sexual embrace while reciting her sacred chant. This form of meditation is obviously a very powerful way of contacting and integrating the feminine aspect of the psyche (the *anima*). A female practitioner uses a male deity in meditation in the same manner to relate to her masculine side (the *animus*).

Aside from the five primordial Buddhas, Buddhist Tantra originally did not give anthropomorphic form to the unmanifested Ultimate Reality. In the 10th century, however, a form of monotheistic god was introduced at the Nalanda Monastery in India. Although developed in the image of a monotheistic god, the Adibuddha (Supreme or First Buddha) does not create the universe, nor is he separate from it. Transcending the duality of form and non-form, he is paradoxically the unity of the two and the progenitor of the five Buddhas. As the primordial Buddha-Mind, the Adibuddha is worshipped as the "root guru" of the Tantric teachings. Different sects have varying representations of the Adibuddha; in the sect I am most familiar with, he begets the name Vajradhara (holder of the vajra scepter, which symbolizes the indestructible diamond-like power of the Void). He appears in several wrathful forms with a consort (Vajra Yogini) as the central deity in assorted advanced Tantric meditation practices.

Vajradhara is sometimes shown in the yabyum (Tantric sexual embrace) posture with Prajnaparamita (see fig. 5 on page 24). As the anthropomorphic representation of the Mahayana text of the same name, Prajnaparamita represents the "Wisdom of the Yonder Shore." According to legend, Buddha hid this book of transcendental knowledge in a heavenly realm until humanity was ready for its profound teachings. An Indian sage, named Nagarjuna, is said to have recouped this scripture in the second century, and the worship of Prajnaparamita became very popular.

The Prajnaparamita scriptures developed the philosophical basis for the teachings on the void nature of Absolute Reality and were the height of the Mahayana doctrine. As a goddess, Prajnaparamita is the voidness that permeates everything – the "emptiness" that gives birth spontaneously to all creation. She was therefore considered by the Mahayana school of Buddhism to be mother of all the Buddhas, because it is through her, empty space-like pristine consciousness, that a Buddha is born. Her Tantric union with Vajradhara symbolically expresses the integration of Tantric "skillful means" with the Mahayana practice of profound meditation on the Void.

In the course of practice, a student of Tantric Buddhism begins by taking refuge in the Buddha (the enlightened mind). The Dharma (the Buddhist doctrine) and the Sangha (community of Buddhist practitioners) are also revered. A lama (literally considered to be an incarnation of the Buddha-Mind) then assigns a patron deity from the Tantric pantheon based on the student's individual needs. If a woman has a lot of repressed anger, one of the wrathful deities may be given. Like a homeopathic remedy,

Figure 5. Vajradhara and Prajnaparamita. The Yabyum posture symbolizes the union of the Supreme Buddha—the primordial power of the Void—and the Mother of all Buddhas—Wisdom Gone Beyond. Contemporary painting by Äge Delbanco reproduced by permission of the artist.

meditation on the wrathful deity will purge the anger from her body-mind. In other instances certain attributes may be acquired from the patron deity. For a man who is lustfully addicted to the beauty of women, a lovely goddess may be employed to transmute those feelings into a more sublime love.

Having realized the qualities embodied in the deity, the lama empowers the student to perform various deity meditations through initiation so that the potentials within the mind of the student are activated. Many years of preliminary practices are normally required before a student is ready to be initiated into a mandala of a higher Tantric deity.

Tantra and
Jungian
Psychology

Though Western psychology has either ignored our spiritual inclinations, or worse, judged them pathological, there is a growing trend toward researching the parapsychological and transpersonal realms of the psyche. Carl Jung was an important pioneer in this quest for a deeper understanding of the nature of the inner self. Breaking from conventional therapeutic orientations, he looked beyond the preoccupation with pathologies and symptoms to the numinous. Venturing into the taboo territory of the mysterious and "divine," his psychotherapy developed into a way of guiding people beyond the narrow confines of ego identity in quest of their wholeness. His findings form a valuable bridge between Tantra and the contemporary transpersonal forms of Western psychology. Before we cross that bridge, let's look at the chasm that separates Tantra and Western psychology.

Western psychology has been traditionally concerned with the treatment of mental illness. Successful treatment is gauged by a person's ability to function "normally" in our social structure. Tantra, on the other hand, focuses on the development of qualities that transcend a mere adaptation to the social norm and aims to heal the major cause of human suffering—the illusion of the ego identity. Furthermore, the concept of the self in Western psychology is based primarily on ego identity. In Tantra, the self has much greater parameters, including its continuity from one life to another, *i.e.*, reincarnation.

Jung describes the ego as a complex of psychic factors and a general awareness of the body that attracts contents from the unconscious and the outside world with which it identifies.[5] Existing only on the surface of ourselves, this self views the world in terms of "I" and the "not I," and cannot, therefore, embrace the experience of transpersonal states of consciousness. The possibility of existing in a state where this separation dissolves, and the familiar "I-ness" is no longer concrete, is unimaginable at best, and frightening at worst in the ego-centered perspective. Nor can this ego-identity trust in its survival of death, or even dramatic periods of transformation. It is firmly bound to its present status by its survival instinct.

As Martin Willson points out in *Rebirth and the Western Buddhist*, in Tantra the belief in the continuity of the mind-stream from one life to the next is the basis for understanding the human condition, and is fundamental to the doctrines of karma and liberation.[6] Karma is the very mechanics of this continuity, and liberation literally means the cessation of the wheel of death and involuntary rebirth. At this time there is convincing scientific evidence

---

[5]Carl Jung, *Analytical Psychology: Its Theory and Practice* (New York: Vintage, 1968), p. 10.
[6]Martin Willson, *Rebirth and the Western Buddhist* (London: Wisdom Publications, 1987), pp. 9–10.

for the doctrine of reincarnation. Dr. Ian Stevenson's research at the University of Virginia, published in *Twenty Cases of Suggestive Reincarnation*,[7] is perhaps the best documented. At any rate, a willingness to consider the possibility and implications of reincarnation is necessary to grasp the essentials of the Tantric orientation.

Next we need to agree upon what we are talking about when we use the words "consciousness" and "psyche," as their meaning in Western psychology is too nebulous or inadequate for our purposes here. In Western psychology, consciousness is the ego-self's awareness; everything that lies beyond it is simply called "unconscious." Furthermore, there is a conflict as to which combination of conscious and unconscious structures constitute the psyche. There are, for example, a great many psychologists who maintain that the psyche is nothing more than biochemical activities in the brain.

Although Jung appreciated the scope and depth of consciousness in some Eastern and primitive cultures, he summed up the common Western view of consciousness as a product of perception and orientation in the external world. He said that it is probably localized in the cerebrum, and speculates that it is an evolution of a sense organ of the skin from our remote ancestors.[8] The Western concept of consciousness implies that without the ego and the cerebrum, consciousness does not exist.

Is it possible that consciousness existed prior to the development of our central nervous system? Is our nervous system growing like a lotus from the mud of the material universe to blossom in the "Light?" Is it possible that consciousness has different qualities in other contexts besides the unique form of it associated with ego and higher brain centers? In Tantra, consciousness is

---

[7]Dr. Ian Stevenson, *Twenty Cases of Suggestive Reincarnation* (Charlottesville, VA: University Press of Virginia, 1974).
[8]Jung, *Analytical Psychology*, pp. 7–8.

experienced on many levels; ego-consciousness is only one of these. In fact, consciousness, in its most sublime condition, is considered the very ground of being itself.

We find a description of five major bodies of consciousness in Tantra. The most sublime, the bliss-body (Anadamayakosa in Hindu Tantra, Buddha in Buddhism), is the part of ourselves rooted in the eternal and infinite dimension of pristine consciousness. Our concept of spirit is the nearest translation we have for this most sublime level of the psyche.

The next subtle body (Vijnanamayakosa, or Vignanam in Buddhism) is similar to our Western notion of the soul. It is the seat of individualized consciousness and contains the potential faculties of spiritual intuition and wisdom.

The third subtle body (Manomayakosa in Hindu Tantra, Kama Manas and Kama Rupa in Buddhism) incorporates our emotional and intellectual natures. These two elements of the psyche function integrally to create the personality. When viewed clairvoyantly, this subtle body is called the aura, and sometimes referred to as the astral and mental bodies respectively.

The fourth body (Pranayamakosa), commonly called the etheric body, is composed of vital energy. This vital body circulates the life force down into, and throughout, the fifth vehicle of consciousness, the physical body (Annamayakosa in Hindu and Sthula Sarira in Buddhist Tantra).

Though existing in different dimensions, each of these sheaths of consciousness is interpenetrated by the one interior to it. Seven vortices of psychic energy—the chakras—traverse these subtle bodies and play an important role in their integration.

The Sanskrit word *chakra* means wheel. A clairvoyant sees the chakras as whirlpools of energy funneling into the etheric body. These etheric centers are, in turn, related to the endocrine glands and major nerve ganglia in the physical body. The chakras translate communications from all levels of the psyche into the electrochemical stimuli of the nervous system and endocrine glands. Conversely, they translate the stimuli of our corporeal self into the language of consciousness of the various subtle bodies. The chakras therefore encompass the entire spectrum of consciousness, from the most primitive (instinctual and sense based) to the most sublime.

Tantric practices are designed to develop all of these levels. When the most sublime body of consciousness is fully integrated into awareness, we become a Buddha (one who has awakened). This experience is called Samadhi in Hindu Tantra. In Sanskrit, *sam* means union, and *adhi* means Lord; thus Samadhi means union with the Lord.

> The Self is the Lord of the self
> and its goal.
>
> (Dharmapala)

I will be using the words psyche and body-mind interchangeably to connote the sum of these bodies of consciousness, including of course the chakra system. Let's begin now to compare Tantra's view of the psyche with Jung's in order to develop the working model that we will employ throughout the rest of the book. In a manner similar to that of the Indian scriptures, Jung recognized a transcendent function in the psyche and called it the *Self*. For Jung this Self was identical with and the source of God-images. Through what Jung called the process of individuation (a progressive assimilation of unconscious contents) the Self becomes more and more conscious. In religious terms, according to Aniela Jaffe in *The Myth of Meaning*, the process of individuation was said by Jung to be "the realization of the Divine within."[9]

By developing the concept of the Self, Jung took a major step toward venturing beyond the confines of the ego identity. Yet the Self in Jung's theory doesn't include the possibility of becoming fully conscious, as does its counterpart in Tantra. Jung's Self is

---

[9]Aniela Jaffe, *The Myth of Meaning* (New York: Penguin, 1975), p. 79.

primarily known indirectly via dreams and other symbolic expressions.

Another important difference is that Jung's concept of the Self implies something that is eternal and yet phenomenal, qualities that are contradictory from the Buddhist viewpoint. Though attempting to embrace the mystery of the union of the opposites, Jung's Self remains in the realm of "thingness," even though he speaks of it as a transcendent function, a uniting symbol, and a whole-making principle, as he struggles to conceptualize his intuition of what he termed "pleroma" in his *Seven Sermons To the Dead*. In this state of pleroma, Jung glimpsed what the Buddhists call the Void, where "nothingness is the same as fullness," and "both thinking and being cease" because that which is absolute has no qualities.[10] But some of the attributes he assigns to the Self betray his intuitive insight.

To research these expressions of the Self, Jung initiated a cross-cultural study of the psyche and discovered universal patterns that he called archetypes. He concluded that these psychic forces were like the genetic code in the physical body; they structurally predetermine the anatomy and function of the psyche. Unless disturbed by personal trauma, they guide the course of individual development. Appearing in dreams, fantasy, art, myth, and religion, and even in scientific thought, the archetypes design the entire field of human experience.

It naturally followed that Jung realized the normally unconscious realms of the psyche consisted of universal as well as personal aspects. Jung came to see our individual identities being formed out of this transpersonal reservoir that he termed the collective unconscious. This inner dimension is of oceanic proportions, and its omnipotent currents and tides surround the shores of space and time that define the island of the ego self. Its

---

[10]Carl Jung, "Septem Sermones ad Mortuos," in *Memories, Dreams, Reflections* (New York: Random House, 1965), p. 397.

horizons stretch back into time immemorial, and forward into future eons. From its depths emerge all of the elements, instincts, desires, conceptual tendencies, and transcendental or spiritual yearnings that have ever been, or will probably ever be, cast onto the shores of human consciousness. In the form of primordial images (archetypes), these psychic structures, with their inherent dualistic expressions (good and evil, light and dark, etc.), provide the framework for the "stuff" of the personal layers of the psyche.

Radmila Moacanin, in *Jung's Psychology and Tibetan Buddhism*, shows how Jung's collective unconscious can be compared to what Buddhists call the "store consciousness" (Alaya-Vijnana).[11] As in the way Jung perceives the collective unconscious to include all human potential and experience, the Alaya-Vijnana is conceived of as a sort of "Universal Mind." Lama Govinda, in *Creative Meditation and Multi-Dimensional Consciousness*, describes this store consciousness as containing primordial forms that embrace the full spectrum of human qualities from the demonic to the divine, and that rise up into other levels of consciousness when triggered by associations.[12]

Continuing to integrate Jung's view of the psyche with that of Tantra's, see if you can imagine the seven chakras unfolding out of the depths of the collective unconscious and rising up through the levels of the personal unconscious and ego consciousness. Through each chakra specific archetypal functions and images are expressed. Together, the seven chakras form the psychic matrix in which the unique form of the body-mind is created.

This generic matrix becomes more characteristically defined as various experiences, and our reactions to them, are established in the recesses of the personal unconscious. The personal uncon-

---

[11]Radmila Moacanin, *Jung's Psychology and Tibetan Buddhism* (London: Wisdom Publications, 1986), p. 75.
[12]Lama Govinda, *Creative Meditation and Multi-Dimensional Consciousness* (Wheaton, IL: Theosophical Publishing House, 1976), p. 30.

scious perceives and acts on emotion/information in a literal way, storing it and directing behavior somewhat like a computer via the autonomic nervous system. The memory of everything that has happened to us, including past lives, is contained here. And, as an interface between the time-space structure of the ego and the other dimensionality of the deeper levels of the psyche, the personal unconscious may also be a sorting house of future contents of ego consciousness.

In general, the personal unconscious has a tendency to remain fixed in the emotional patterns and belief structures that make a deep impression on it. Many fears and self-limiting behaviors stem from such unconscious conditioning. These effects in the personal level of the unconscious obscure the positive functions of the archetypes and cause us to become either fixated on certain archetypal images, or vulnerable to their darker side.

In Tantric terms, the impact of past experiences, desires, and actions (including mental actions) are embedded as karmic seeds in the body-mind. If these seeds are not uprooted, they will continue to bear their bitter fruit in spite of conscious efforts to prevent them. Each chakra contains any number of seed patterns from past experiences – related to archetypal motifs – which define the unconscious parameters of the ego-self. Referred to as obscuration in Buddhist Tantra, these seed patterns (Samskaras) eclipse the wisdom-energy acting through any particular chakra and are major obstacles to the realization of our Buddha nature.

Next, the chakras emerge into the sphere of the ego consciousness. The rational mind is capable of more complex functions than the personal unconscious; it can reason inductively as well as deductively. It can also repress desires and memories that it does not want to acknowledge. Thus, it enjoys some degree of autonomy from the personal and transpersonal unconscious realms. But in order to maintain the desperate illusion of its sovereignty, it is prone to rationalize. In each of the chakras then, we may find distorted images of reality that the conscious self uses to order, and perhaps manipulate, the world within and without to conform to its desires and preconceptions.

The rational self can be quite stubborn, but it is relatively easy to reeducate. Reading a book like this one may be enough to convince the rational mind of its need to alter existing attitudes and ideas. Unfortunately, the deprogramming and reeducation of the personal unconscious requires much more skill and time. But unless this task is successfully accomplished, conscious desires to change will most often prove ineffectual. Optimally, the rational and personal unconscious minds must harmonize their efforts and attune themselves to the deeper levels of the collective unconscious.

Each chakra can be visualized as a lens in a slide projector in which certain generic functions of the psyche are brought to light. For instance, the theme of the first chakra is the survival and well-being of the physical body; it is associated with the most primitive or instinctual level of the psyche. The carousel of slides in the first chakra would, therefore, contain personalized archetypal images of this level portraying a well-adjusted orientation, a deprived and traumatic scenario, or a curious mixture of both.

The sum total of "slide collections" in all of the chakras creates the illusion of our individual identity. These slide collections can be related to the bundle of aggregates (the skandhas of form, feeling, cognition, mental volition, and consciousness) that, in Buddhist terms, compose the sense of the ego-self.

In our modern culture, our "slide collections" are gorged with erroneous effigies that clamor for our attention while the ego-self is drastically alienated from the sources of spiritual nourishment deep within the psyche. We live in a synthetic world divorced from nature within and without. Like the prodigal son, we have forgotten our true heritage and the purpose of our journey in consciousness.

When we embark on this journey, either consciously or through inner prompting, we confront things beneath our "civilized" veneers that we would just as soon avoid. Hence the process of individuation, in Jungian therapy, and the Tantric practice of transforming the deluded aspects of the ego-self into their wisdom-energies often proves to be a painful one.

Contacting the primordial power of the archetypes can also be terrifying to the ego-self and Jung maintained a healthy respect for their "uncontrollable" potentials. Tantric legends are full of miraculous claims for the awakening of Kundalini, or the Dumo-fire. Merely awakening this power, however, does not automatically insure spiritual perfection. This primordial power may indeed be venomous, activating unconscious contents which may cause severe psychological imbalances if not diligently assimilated. Tibetans say that arousing the fire is like putting a snake in a hollow bamboo stick; it can only go one of the two ways, up or down.

The work begins, then, with befriending and clearing irrelevant or self-inhibiting contents of the personal unconscious. Before we can deprogram the unconscious it is often necessary to become aware of the initial influences. Reexperiencing these dissolves their crystallized emotional/conceptual formations lodged in any particular chakra.[13]

To understand and communicate with the unconscious, it is important to realize that it is powered by emotional dynamics and "thinks" in terms of images and symbols. The metaphorical qualities of dreams and mythology readily illustrate this.

Another important thing to consider is that this level of the psyche does not normally discern between "reality" and imagination. The use of hypnosis, active imagination, dream work, and guided imagery demonstrate how the unconscious mind can be tapped and changed through metaphor and visualization. In fact,

---

[13]For more information on reprogramming the unconcious mind, I highly recommend *Software for the Mind*, by Emmett E. Miller, MD. (Berkeley, CA: Celestial Arts, 1987).

advertising companies are making millions of dollars a year exploiting techniques of subliminal communication.

In Tantra, meditation produces alpha and theta brain wave frequencies which give us access to areas of the psyche outside of the normal rational functions. It is here in these subliminal levels that the images and ritual activities of Tantra work their magic. The Tantric deities can be thought of as ornate cultural renditions of the timeless archetypes. In addition to the power of the numinous depths of the psyche that they contain, they can be experienced as batteries of psychic energy charged with the potent meditations of Tantric yogis for well over a thousand years. This potential is tapped and used to transform the body-mind into a clear vessel for transpersonal forces in Tantric practices.

Likewise, the purpose of Jungian therapy is not merely to treat symptoms, but to enhance the whole-making functions of the body-mind. This begins with a gradual softening of ego boundaries so that repressed contents are assimilated by the ego-self. This process leads to further integration of archetypal elements from the more universal depths of the psyche. Healing the split between the conscious and unconscious transforms the ego into a more transpersonal form of identity.

Jung pursued an open-ended, client-centered approach in his therapeutic methods. He recognized the uniqueness of each individual and followed his patient's own inner guidance along the path to wholeness. Like our "Buddha Nature," Jung had the conviction that the Self possesses the wisdom and intent of leading us to our true nature, if we would only relinquish our resistance and hubris.

The goal of Jungian therapy, as well as many of its methods and concepts, are reminiscent of ancient Tantric practices. Jung's recognition of the mandala as an expression of the Self, the value of working with the symbolic manifestations of the psyche via dream work and active imagination, the appreciation for the reconciliation of opposites within the psyche (male and female, conscious and unconscious etc.) and the clearing of the contents of the personal unconscious to gain access to the manna of the archetypes, are all easily related to Tantric procedures.

Though Tantra is a more radical system for the transfiguration of the body-mind, Jung's courageous explorations and profound insight provide us Westerners with some very useful concepts to begin to comprehend the wisdom in Tantric symbols, myths, and meditation rituals.

Like the process of individuation, the way of Tantra requires courage, honesty, willingness to change, and disciplined freedom. The humility and focus on priorities needed to tread this path are not easily acquired, nor sustained, in our modern times. The Buddhists warn us, however, that entering the Tantric path without the necessary commitment is like trying to whip butter from water.

Before going on to some "hands on experience" of Jungian psychology and Tibetan Tantra, demonstrated in the functions of the chakras, there is one thought that would be helpful to keep in mind. Though presented here in a sequential order, the inner realities of the psyche are best understood in terms of the time and space qualities of dreams. Each chakra is embedded in the transpersonal depths of the psyche, the archetypes and related stages of development do not necessarily emerge within the narrow confines of linear time, they can rise up to the surface at any time from any depth.

Bon voyage!

CHAPTER
TWO

♦

THE CAVE OF
THE
ANCIENTS

*O*n the floor of the pelvis, from the base of the spine to the genitals, is a realm called the egg of Brahma in Hindu Tantra. In some Hindu myths, Brahma is the god of creation, and the egg of Brahma can be correlated to the archetypal theme of the world egg. Found universally in mythology, the primal womb, or the world egg, are common symbols for the original wholeness from which all life is derived.

The first chakra, called Muladhara (root support) in Hindu Tantra, is located in the center of this egg. It is especially important in meditation because the creative force of the cosmos lies dormant here in the mythic form of the Serpent Goddess Kundalini. The image of the serpent evokes a rich mosaic of symbols connected with the fertile earth, the ageless wisdom, and the regenerative powers of the deeper layers of the psyche.

Inside the lotus of the root chakra, which has four crimson petals, there is a yellow square that represents the earth element. Inside of this there is a white elephant with seven trunks. See fig. 6 on page 38. In India, albino elephants are thought to attract their celestial relatives, clouds. These heavenly elephants bring the rain that enables Mother Earth to be fertile and abundant. Elephants therefore bestow earthly blessings and good fortune.

In Buddhist Tantra, the chakra system is likened to a sacred temple with five stories. Each level of the temple contains a throne and a mandala of one of the five Primordial Buddhas. The first chakra, on the ground floor, is symbolized by a yellow square and associated with the earth element. Lama Govinda, in *Foundations of Tibetan Mysticism*, says that the Buddhists correlate the earth element with the realm of karmic law because it is the plane on which the seeds of our actions ripen. It is also the domain of bondage to form, which is qualified by the forces of rigidity and

Figure 6. Muladhara. The first chakra has four crimson petals that symbolize the four kinds of bliss experienced when Kundalini awakens. Inside the lotus we find a yellow square, mandala for the Earth Element. Within it we see the seed mantra LAM, which invokes the ancient deity Indra. The white elephant is Indra's vehicle and a symbol for prosperity. We also see an inverted triangle, the yoni which represents the female genitals and the feminine power of creation. Within it Kundalini is shown coiled three and one-half times around the lingam.

inertia.[1] The Primordial Buddha Amoghasiddhi sits on the throne of the first chakra. See fig. 7 on page 40. Although he is normally connected to the air element and the color green, it is his All-Accomplishing Wisdom (karma-free or spontaneous activity derived from the realization of the inseparableness of the Void and the appearance of phenomenal reality) that can best transform the forces of the body-mind functioning through the first chakra. Amoghasiddhi's deluded passion is jealousy or envy based on the fear or anxiety that we may fail to accomplish our goals, or that others might achieve more than we do.

In general, the primary function of the root chakra is to translate the life force into the survival needs and activities of the physical organism. The feelings of security and confidence in the physical world instill in us the trust necessary for the positive expression of the root chakra. Without this sense of feeling safe in the body and the physical environment, a deep fear undermines all other levels of consciousness.

Aside from past life influences, the personal elements in the first chakra are primarily derived from prenatal and birth experiences. Parental and home environment naturally follow as important factors in determining the basis for our orientation toward the world. Psychologists generally agree that we learn more in our first year of life than we do during all the years that follow. If our prenatal and early environment satisfied our needs for food, warmth, sense of belonging, and protection, then a trust of our external environment was established. If, on the other hand, the environment of the womb and early infancy were emotionally cold, nonsupportive, or disruptive, then the impressions in the first chakra interpret the world and human beings as threatening or alien.

---

[1]Lama Govinda, *Foundations of Tibetan Mysticism* (York Beach, ME: Samuel Weiser, 1974; and London: Rider & Co., 1974), p. 181.

Figure 7. Amoghasiddhi is the Lord of the root chakra and embodies the All-Encompassing Wisdom. His color is green and he rules the Air Element. His right hand is raised in the Abhaya Mudra, casting the blessing of fearlessness. Illustration is Plate 7 from *Foundations of Tibetan Mysticism*, by Lama Govinda (published in 1974 by Samuel Weiser, York Beach, Maine, and Rider & Co., London) and is reproduced by permission of the publishers.

It is usually difficult to unearth first chakra influences because they were programmed during fetal development and early infancy, essentially preconscious periods. Unconscious acceptance of "what has always been" and the fear of severing our psychological roots work against the reconstruction of reality at this fundamental level.

The archetypal aspects of the first chakra are rooted in the most primitive realms of the psyche, connecting us to the time when we existed in instinctual rapport with Mother Nature. See fig. 8. In this preconscious era we were united to the unconscious processes of nature. Erich Neumann, in *The Origin and History of Consciousness*, shows how this initial stage of development, relived in infancy (in addition to the world egg), is often symbolized in circular motifs which point to our original wholeness—they are without beginning and end, self-contained and eternal. The

Figure 8. Uroborus. A dragon eating its own tail, a medieval symbol for the self-contained and whole-making qualities of the psyche. From a French drawing from the 13th century.

psyche and the world were not yet split in two by the ego identity in this preconscious state.[2]

Neumann goes on to say that ever since we were expelled from the womb of the unconscious, we have longed to return to Paradise Lost, the state of being devoid of conscious pain and pleasure and responsible actions. The Garden of Eden myth dramatizes our dread and reluctance to emerge as conscious, and consequently separate, beings. The unconscious state seemed to be our natural condition. To awaken required great effort and the painful awareness of duality.[3]

It is here in the root chakra, then, that we find our first obstacle to the development of consciousness, the inertia and clinging embrace of the unconscious. Freud was fascinated by this regressive tendency in the psyche and named it the death wish. Ironically enough, for the world of opposites are quite comfortable existing side by side here in this level of the psyche, the forces of self-formation and survival are also generated here in the instincts of the first chakra.

In Tantric symbology, the first chakra embodies the qualities of the earth element, such as solidity and inertia. In daily life, the first chakra covers these concerns: how we relate to and take care of our physical bodies (nutrition, exercise, and gratification of the senses), how we earn our living and maintain a shelter, our attitude toward money and the quality of our physical environment, how we relate to the sensual world and material possessions, and our ability to trust and feel safe on the physical plane. In addition to parental and environmental imprints from this life, conditions and traumas experienced in past lives may affect the flow of psychic energy through the first chakra and the resulting view of physical reality. Often severe trauma or injury to the physical

---

[2]Erich Neumann, *The Origins and History of Consciousness*, Bollingen Series, Vol. XLII (Princeton, NJ: Princeton University Press, 1954), p. 8.
[3]Neumann, *The Origins and History of Consciousness*, pp. 114–116, 280

body in previous incarnations will manifest itself as related symptoms in this life, or cause crippling unconscious fears and behaviors.

◇

Being in the Body

"Being in your body" and "being grounded" are popular phrases today. What do they mean and how do they relate to the first chakra? In a very literal sense, the body is a living sculpture of yourself. Aside from genetic inheritance and the body images received in childhood, the body is molded by changes in the psychological state. Thoughts and feelings as psychic energy in the aura affect the physical body via nerve centers and endocrine glands, altering its apparent structure and function. Some examples of this are: the drastic physical changes in appearance which are clearly seen in people subject to multiple personalities, and the superhuman strength experienced in emergencies or under hypnosis.

On the cellular level, the processes that maintain a whole and healthy body are constantly disrupted by a war between actions, emotions and concepts. For example, when emotions are triggered (sexual excitement, crying, anger), energy begins to flow from the emotional body into the physical, preparing it for action. The ego says "No!" and the action is suppressed. "No" means contraction in the body—the muscles tighten, the breath becomes shallow, and the body is frozen in conflict.

Most of us have grown up with these chronic tension patterns. In response to unexpressed emotion, the body constricts as it becomes more and more segregated from the conscious mind.

This repression of awareness in the body protects us from unacceptable feelings, but it also curtails vitality and pleasurable feelings. The more this state of affairs is taken for granted, the more abandoned the body becomes. We deprive ourselves of what we need to grow and thrive and wonder why we do not feel physically vital.

The contemporary wave of bodywork techniques clearly demonstrates the protean qualities of the body. Blocked emotions and inner tensions can be released and the body can become free, loose, and healthy; in some instances changing its appearance and structure quite drastically. In addition to the release of blocked pain and frozen emotions, the ability to experience pleasure in the body can be re-established.

Our bodies are animals. They need exercise, good food, and a supportive environment; they also need loving touch and intimacy. Touch is a very basic need. For the infant, it is just as necessary as food. Infants who are not cuddled and touched may become listless, lose their appetites, waste away, and even die.

Adults may find themselves seeking to fulfill the need to touch and be touched through sexual interaction. We forget that touching does not necessarily have to be associated with sexuality, and we may severely limit our opportunities to receive and give nurturing.

On the other hand, the instinctive drive to mate and reproduce is also associated with the first chakra. For this reason, the first chakra has often been called the sex chakra. Sex, however, does not pertain solely to one chakra, since it is sexual energy (*i.e.*, libido, Kundalini) that flows up through each chakra. We will see how this energy is transformed, assuming different qualities in each chakra.

The nature of sexual energy in the first chakra is explained graphically by Dane Rudhyar, in *Occult Preparations for a New Age*. It is tied to bio-cultural purposes; it is a functional and instinctual compulsion rooted in the collective unconscious. He offers the image of a man tilling the soil, satisfied by muscular release and fruitful work, and compares it to the husbanding of the woman's earth-nature to create offspring.[4]

The drive to reproduce—that dominates the sexual energy in the first chakra—can also be seen as a projection of individual identity into physical objects. Through investing psychic energy into offspring, artistic creations, and material possessions, we ritualistically attempt to ensure solidity and continuity of our sense of self. Instinctually, we seek a sense of belonging and security in the physical world. Like the dog that defends its territory, we cling desperately to the sense of "mine" that we project onto these objects.

In *The Mythic Image*, Joseph Campbell compares the nature of Kundalini here at this level of the psyche to mythological dragons which are prone to hoard and guard things. They often hoard things that they cannot even use—usually beautiful young maidens and treasures. Nonetheless, they hang on to and guard them so their inherent values are never realized.[5]

In mythological lore, the hero (ego consciousness) will eventually have to meet and conquer this dragon in order to rescue the maiden and acquire the treasure. In the Tantric legend of the Goddess Kundalini, we find the valuable vital energy being held captive by the unconscious instincts in the first chakra. Like the mythological hero, a Tantric yogi must release Kundalini so she may ascend through the chakras and reveal all her treasures of consciousness. Both the hero and yogi have to journey into the bowels of the Earth and confront the dark forces there in order to realize those qualities that bring forth a higher meaning and fulfillment in life.

---

[4]Dane Rudhyar, *Occult Preparations for a New Age* (Wheaton, IL: Theosophical Publishing House, 1975), pp. 144–145.

[5]Joseph Campbell, *The Mythic Image*, Bollingen Series, Vol. C (Princeton, NJ: Princeton University Press, 1981), p. 341.

The corporeal body is a vehicle, it needs to be maintained and its potentials actualized. A healthy body is the first step to the vast dimensions of awareness beyond the ordinary mind. In Tibetan Tantra, the body is not seen as a fixed thing, it is an expression of continual incarnation. Who we are, what we are thinking and feeling, and unconscious activities are embodied every moment. Changes in the psyche mobilize forces that are concretely manifested in the body.

◇

Grounding

With a closed or traumatized first chakra, the conscious self is cut off from the body and is, therefore, unaware of its needs. The term "spaced-out" is commonly used to describe this state of disembodiment. In this ungrounded condition, life is experienced as a struggle and one feels unable to cope with reality. On the other hand, "a sense of presence" is a phrase used to describe being dynamically focused in the body.

Another way of looking at grounding is to compare the self to a sensitive radio receiver which requires a grounding wire to alleviate static. When we are grounded, psychic energy flows from the more subtle levels of the psyche into the physical body. This helps us resist influences in the environment. If the first chakra is blocked, the circuit is incomplete and the auric field is greatly weakened. In this state, we become anxious and are more easily influenced by the thoughts and emotions of others.

The wave particles that oscillate in space to create the appearance of the physical dimension vibrate within a certain electromagnetic frequency (7.8 Hz). Through the first chakra it is possible, in fact vitally necessary, to go into sympathy with the pulse of the terrestrial field. Being locked into it is another way to explain the term grounding.

Biological processes function best within the natural electromagnetic frequencies of the earth. Variations from these natural frequencies cause stress in biological systems, eventually leading to degeneration of organs and tissues. In addition to air, water, and food pollution, the increasing electromagnetic pollution of our technological society is becoming a real health hazard. Radio, TV, and microwaves, high power lines and domestic electrical wiring, to mention a few, are all sources of disturbances in the body's electromagnetic field. Chaotic vibrations in the aura, or an overabundance of beta brain wave frequencies (associated with the rational mind and states of worry, fear, etc.) also disrupt the electromagnetic field of the body.

For most people, psychic energy is scattered frantically through the mental and emotional bodies. Seldom is there peace and clarity. The mind is always busy, jumping from one train of thought to another, from one worry, problem, or scheme to another. The emotional body is usually buffeted like a small boat on a tumultuous sea, and the physical organism exists within this aura of chaotic vibrations. It is forced to respond continually to conflicting stimuli impinging upon the nervous and glandular systems from these various levels of the psyche.

When the aura and the physical body relax into resonance with the terrestrial magnetic field, tranquil theta and alpha brain wave frequencies are naturally produced and a deep sense of peace prevails. The magnetic field of the body is once again nourished and embraced by the mother geomagnetic field. We feel safe and protected. Biofeedback, meditation, and self-hypnosis are a few of the techniques that can be used to relax the body-mind into resonance with the earth's magnetic field.

Let's entertain another perspective to further expand the connotations of the grounding experience. The Garden of Eden was not a place, but a state of consciousness: We began our journey by being cast out of our unconscious and instinctual rapport with Mother Nature. As exemplified in the lives of spiritually realized persons, we can return to that garden consciously. Once the unfoldment of consciousness is completed, we return to our original unity. Becoming the whole living through the part, we experience intimately and consciously our groundedness in the cosmic organism. Its wholeness lives in us; it is our life.

$$\Diamond$$

The Parental Matrix

Physically, we are conceived from the biological union of mother and father. Psychologically, we are born from the Great Polarity. Behind the mask of the personal mother and father are the two primordial archetypes of the Great Mother and Father. As infants, we sought the nurturing and guidance inherent in these psychological progenitors through relationship to our biological parents.

In childhood we instinctively compared our objective parents to the internal "ideal" parental archetypes. The fundamental need to relate to and be nourished, protected, and guided by the Great Mother and Father was often painfully frustrated by the inadequacies of our biological parents. As a result, we felt deprived and grew to mistrust and even resent our biological parents, and often the world they represent.

The emotional complexes that children develop, and the psychological values absorbed from the parental environment create barriers to growth. Unless they are overcome, these barriers will affect the foundation of the entire process of development.

Everyone, at the deepest level, needs to feel loved and supported by his or her parents. When we feel that we were denied that love, we try to fill the emptiness in numerous ways. We are either driven by this deprivation or controlled by compensatory defenses. A healthy relationship to the Mother and Father archetypes is buried within–beneath layers of pain and defenses. It is important to divulge these layers of trauma. Cathartic therapies, such as Rebirthing and Deep Tissue Bodywork, active imagination, Jungian dreamwork, and various orthodox psychoanalytic approaches, are some methods for accessing and releasing these unconscious factors. The Buddhist practice of insight meditation, to be discussed in a later chapter, is another effective way to penetrate into these depths of the psyche.

Through these psychological excavations, we can reach down through the layers of psychic energy that exist below our reactions to parental influences. As we unearth these hidden factors, and begin to own our own feelings and projections, we start to feel compassion for ourselves and for our parents. We are then less likely to blame our parents and more ready to open ourselves to their gifts of love and loyalty, no matter how small and imperfect. Only then can we begin to root ourselves in the deeper levels of the psyche to tap the nourishment of the Great Mother and Father.

In the acorn the whole oak tree slumbers. In a similar way the polarity of the Great Mother and Father contains all the potential for the development of consciousness. Its unfoldment is dependent on our changing relationship to these archetypes, which are first projected onto the biological parents and later onto gods and goddesses who become our spiritual parents.

◇

Psychic Reading
of the Root
Chakra

An example of a psychic reading of the first chakra will serve to
summarize many of the topics we have discussed thus far:

> Clairvoyantly focusing attention on his first chakra, I
> sense tightness. From this constricted energy, I get an
> impression of fear, timidity, and suspicion. At a deeper
> level, I am aware of feelings of anger.
>
> Tuning in more carefully to these feelings, images
> begin to appear. Focusing on one of these, I see a fetus
> in the womb during labor. It is struggling for its life
> against the reluctance of the mother to give birth. The
> mother does not want the child; she is unhappy with her
> husband; her life is a struggle. All these forces are
> impinging on the infant as it fights for its right to be born
> and live. The mother is finally drugged and the birth
> forced. Heart pounding and fear racing through its veins,
> the infant is thrust into a cold, bright environment, han-
> dled roughly, and then taken away and left alone.
>
> Another image appears now. Acting out of frustration
> and resentment, the mother is refusing to take care of
> the child's physical needs—feeding, diaper changing, etc.
> The child feels abandoned and unwanted. The repeated
> experience of hunger that goes unheeded by the mother
> instills in the child's body a sense of fear and mistrust.
>
> Now I see the mother acting with hostility toward the
> child, venting anger at her own life. The child shrinks in
> fear at these attacks; unable to understand and protect

itself, it feels helpless. The child's body withdraws and hardens against the repeated and arbitrary hostility.

In another image, the mother is deep in thought. She is scheming to leave her husband. She is torn about the child; she thinks it would hurt the father if she took the child, and this pleases her. But she doesn't really want the child; and she gets pleasure from imagining the father having to change diapers, etc. She is full of malice and revenge. The child is immersed in this environment of hatred and senses impending separation and abandonment. Without understanding all the causes and circumstances, the child unconsciously identifies with this chaos of feelings.

We could go on to look at the father's relationship to the child and the mother, his sense of responsibility, or his attitude toward his work. All these factors would have some influence on the child's relationship to the physical world. However, the above reading is sufficient to illustrate how psychic imprints influence the first chakra. You can imagine how these might affect the development of the child and its later experiences in life.

We need to free ourselves from the "personalities" of our parents, rather than remaining stuck in blaming them for not being everything that we wanted them to be. People who are "still mad at mommy" should not work with Kundalini, for they may be overwhelmed with anger because the ego is still fixated at a frustrated infantile stage of development. We need to purge the self-images that we adopted in the mirror of parental actions and attitudes and become people in our own right.

◇

Going for
Refuge

After meditating on the human situation, Gautama Buddha concluded that life was conditioned by suffering. All life is in flux, and trying to establish something solid and permanent leads to suffering. Feeling attached to how we would like things to be and having aversions to how things are is the cause of all this suffering. At the root of attachment and aversion is the phenomenon of the ego-identity. When Buddha awoke from the dream of this ego-identity, he began to teach that we can overcome the causes of suffering by right understanding, right thought, right speech, right action, right livelihood, right effort, right mindfulness, and right concentration.

The Buddhist path begins with taking refuge. In the traditional setting, a lama initiates a new student in a refuge ceremony. Going to refuge is a symbolic way of acknowledging that we are alienated from the true self and that we are entrusting ourselves to the guidance of the Awakened-Mind within us.

In Tantric Buddhism, taking refuge has more specific meanings. When the psychic channels in the body are purified, they become an Emanation Body of the Buddha-Mind. The vital winds, or psychic energies, that flow through these channels are, when cleansed, an Enjoyment Body. And the purified sexual fluids are a Truth Body. When we appreciate these three elements as the Three Bodies of the Awakened-Mind, we take the vajra refuge (*vajra* means diamond-like or indestructible).

After the initial refuge ceremony, the practitioner begins each meditation session with a refuge visualization. Before beginning to meditate, the most important factor is our attitude. A correct understanding of the refuge is based on the faith in the unfolding of our own true nature. Along with conviction we need lucidity; we are meditating to realize Buddhahood. Faith, clarity, and resolution to stay focused on the goal, and the means to attain the goal—these are the basis of the refuge and the proper attitude for meditation.

In Tibet there is a saying that "directing the mind is like bridling a fine horse to make him rideable."[6] The body, speech and mind, like a wild horse, contain powerful energies that can be harnessed for constructive work. We can learn to direct these forces in our morning meditation.

Buddhists of all sects honor daily the Triple Gem—the Buddha (the Awakened-Mind), the Dharma (the teachings), and the Sangha (the community of Buddhist practitioners). The followers of the Vajrayana (Tantric Buddhism) also add homage to their guru, who embodies the lineage of teachers stretching back to Buddha himself. The practitioner invokes these four concrete manifestations of the Enlightened-Mind for direction and support in daily meditations.

The meditation that follows is a rendition of the refuge visualization adapted for our purpose here. It has been combined with the initial step to mastery of meditation, called samatha. The Tibetan word for *samatha* is zhignas, and means to dwell in peace. It refers to the development of one-pointedness, which frees the mind from the distractions of thoughts. These two practices are the root support of Tibetan Tantra.

---

[6]Lama Thubten Yeshe, *Wisdom-Energy* (Honolulu: Conch Press, 1976), p. 74.

Figure 9. Shakyamuni Buddha. A meditational deity used in the refuge ceremony symbolizing the commitment to reaching the goal of Enlightenment. From the Thanka collection of Sergei Diakoff. Reproduced by permission.

◇

Shakyamuni
Buddha
Meditation

Begin by placing your body in a meditational posture. Relax and focus your awareness on your breathing. Allow the breath to be full, continuous, and effortless. You may want to regulate your breath by silently repeating Shakyamuni Buddha's mantra: OM TA YA THA MUNI MUNI MAHAMUNYE SVAHA (asceticism or control, greatest asceticism, so be it). Using a count of four for the inhale and exhale, recite OM TA YA THA on the inhale, MUNI MUNI on the exhale, MAHAMUNYE on the next inhale, and SVA-HA on the last exhale. It is also helpful to be aware of your first chakra; feel it relaxing, opening, and grounding you as you focus on the breath and mantra.

As you become more and more relaxed, begin to visualize Shakyamuni seated before you. See fig. 9 on page 54. Imagine him meditating beneath the bodhi tree, where after many years of wandering and searching for the way to liberation, he vowed to remain in meditation until he reached enlightenment. His complexion is golden and he wears saffron-colored monk's robes. In his left hand he holds a bowl filled with the nectar that destroys the four hindrances, which Buddha has already overcome: the suffering of our aggregates, the demon of death, our disturbing unsubdued minds, and the demon of desire. His right hand is touching the earth because when Lord Buddha sat beneath the bodhi tree, the temptress Mara Kama Deva came to tempt him. She tried to persuade him from his goal of enlightenment. But no matter what means Mara used, Buddha was unmoved from his meditation. Touching the earth, he asked it to witness how he was not disturbed by the temptress. The earth trembled and

Figure 10. OM AH HUNG. Seed mantras visualized in the head, throat, and heart chakras to purify body, speech, and mind.

shook six times to answer, thus the meaning of the Earth-Touching Mudra.

Next gaze upon his face, experience the depth of his tranquility. And then notice how motionless and relaxed his body is. Like a stone, it rests solidly on the ground. Contemplate the Guru Shakyamuni Buddha as a fully enlightened being who has infinite compassion, patience, and the knowledge to lead all beings out of suffering to the path of liberation. Pleading with him to bestow his wisdom and compassion on you, pray in your own words to have the hinderances in your mind and heart removed. Then vow to refrain from those actions of body, speech, and mind that would become obstacles on the path to enlightenment. And finally pray to awaken to the Buddha Nature for the benefit of all sentient beings.

Visualize a white OM on his forehead, a red AH at his throat, and blue HUM in his heart. The light rays coming from these three syllables are the essence and power of the Wisdom and Compassion of Buddha's sacred body, speech, and mind, respectively. As the white light from the OM shines into your own sixth chakra, all negative energies in the body are purified. As the red light from the AH shines into your own fifth chakra, all impurities of speech are cleansed. The blue light from the HUM clarifies all delusions from your Mind-Heart.[7] (See fig. 10.)

After receiving this empowerment from Shakyamuni, feel yourself sinking into a deeper and deeper state of meditation. Deeper and deeper, until you reach the depth of Buddha's concentration. As this happens, Buddha's image dissolves into you. You are transformed into Buddha seated beneath the bodhi tree in the Earth-Touching Mudra. Your body is stable and fixed like a stone, and you are absorbed in tranquil meditation. Allowing your awareness to sink like a heavy weight to the floor of your pelvis,

---

[7]For more information on the Refuge practice, refer to Khetsun Sangpo Rinbochay, *Tantric Practice in Nying-Mapa* (Ithaca, NY: Snow Lion, 1982).

feel yourself continuing to sink into deeper and deeper levels of inner peace while you simply remain attentive to the breath coming in and going out of your nostrils.

If any distracting thoughts should arise, gently bring your awareness back to this image of yourself and continue to focus on your breathing.

As you continue to settle, you can imagine that you are going down through the depths of your inner self. From the turmoil of the surface of your mind, you are descending down into the calm depths of the sea of consciousness within. As you continue to breathe and relax, you sink deeper and deeper into this sea of consciousness, where you calmly abide in a wonderful serene state of meditation. Remain in this peace as long as you like.

Before arising from meditation, mentally go through the day that lies before you, seeing yourself abiding in this calm and clear state of awareness. As you view yourself in specific situations, choose certain aspects of those situations as reminders. See yourself becoming aware of these reminders and remembering this state of tranquility and your commitment to Buddhahood. As you go through this day ahead of you, see and feel yourself acting like a Buddha.

CHAPTER
THREE

♦

HER SPECIAL
ABODE

*T*he Hindu diagram for the second chakra has six vermilion petals. Inside its lotus there is a crescent moon–luminous white, cool, and receptive–which symbolizes the water element. Within the crescent moon we find Makara, the monster of the deep who lives at the bottom of the sea.

The Sanskrit name for the second chakra is Svadhisthana, meaning "her special abode" (or place of pleasure). It is interesting, and significant, that the ancient yogis would associate the second chakra with the special domain of the serpent goddess, as her appearance here displays many mythological elements of the Great Mother. Portrayed with prominent amorous, generative, dominating, and sometimes ruthless qualities, the Great Mother is connected with cults of fertility and sexual orgies, as well as images that depict the inimical forces of the unconscious. All of these factors are found in the Hindu mythology of the second chakra. (See fig. 11 on page 60.)

The second chakra is located between the navel and the pubic bone. Psychologically, it relates to the pre-rational and dream-like stages of consciousness, where no stable identity has yet been established. Neumann points out in *The Origins and*

History of Consciousness that this stage of development is symbolized in world mythology by youthful fertility gods. Lacking heroic
strengths, they are powerless and suffer a collective fate at the
hands of the Great Mother Goddess. Fertility cults, in which the
ritual male was sometimes sacrificed, were typical dramatizations
of this layer of the psyche.[1] In the process of opening the second
chakra, therefore, we may confront deep-seated fears and ambivalent sexual feelings as some of these archaic elements of the
collective unconscious become more apparent in our personal
lives.

During the first several years of infancy, we live through a
stage very similar to the historical period related to the mythology

Figure 11. The second chakra, Svadhisthana. Within the lotus of six
vermillion petals is a white crescent symbolizing the Water Element.
The seed mantra VAM invokes the ancient deity Varuna, Lord of the
Sea. Varuna's vehicle is Makara, a monster who lives at the bottom of
the sea.

---

[1]Erich Neumann, *The Origins and History of Consciousness*, Bollingen Series, Vol.
XLII (Princeton, NJ: Princeton University Press, 1954), pp. 39–102.

of the Great Mother. We saw in the first chakra how, as infants, we ideally learn to trust the world when our survival needs are met during the prenatal and first years of life. After this time we begin to differentiate ourselves from mother and environment. In doing so, we experience our own helplessness and powerlessness. Our dependence on the mothering parent naturally becomes associated with our survival in a new way—to survive is to be loved, to be lovable. This gives us some insight into the anxiety and incredible "charge" that we carry with us into our present relationships, and the devastating insecurity that results from rejection and loneliness.

In the second chakra level of development we are awakening to a consciousness of feelings. Our feeling awareness is primarily concerned with pleasurable or painful reactions to the world. A person fixated in an unconscious second chakra is therefore pre-occupied with pleasure/pain reactions. This leads to an addiction to pleasurable experiences and a compulsion to avoid unpleasant ones. This motivation differs from that of mere survival found in the first chakra, but it is an equal source of anxiety. The sense of the self here in the second chakra is hence defined by the totality of objects, persons, and situations that make us feel emotionally secure or that are associated with pleasure. Or, in a negative sense, those things that are connected to pain and insecurity.

In terms of the sexual energy associated with pleasure and pain in the second chakra, there are two basic ways of dealing with it. One is to continue to allow this energy to flow through the second chakra while letting go of past fears, disillusionments, and romantic expectations. A more extreme approach, recommended by many spiritual traditions, is to avoid sexual experiences. Though denial may be beneficial at certain times, eventually all the old scars and fears here will need to be healed so the "waters of life" can flow through the second chakra and into all levels of the psyche.

Carrying the connotation of sexuality, psychic energy in the second chakra plays an important role in the magnetism that draws male to female. This magnetism is intimately connected to the projection of the archetypes of animus and anima, Jungian terms for the masculine and feminine counterparts of the psyche.

The second chakra also has a special relationship to the etheric body. As a force field of vital energies, the etheric body is an interface between the physical and subtle bodies. Currents of life force run through it and into the physical body in myriad rushing streams. These currents have a nurturing and cleansing effect, and are correlated with the spleen, lymph, and urinary systems. Their courses are mapped and manipulated by methods such as Polarity Therapy, Acupuncture, and Taoist and Tantric meditation techniques. The free flow of these currents is essential to the health and vitality of the physical body.

The etheric body is an impressionable and receptive medium that reverberates in response to emotions in the astral world. The second chakra plays a primary role in translating these impulses to the nervous system. Not only are our own feelings felt in the second chakra, but emotional forces in the environment are also received. This sensitivity can be very confusing and disruptive, especially when it functions below the level of awareness, as it normally does.

Because the rational mind is uncomfortable with painful or powerful feelings, the second chakra is often quite blocked. Sexual and romantic desires, loneliness, feelings of vulnerability, desperation, the longing to feel loved and emotionally secure, and resentment and anger for being deprived of these needs, are some common feelings found in the second chakra when its contents surface into awareness.

When the second chakra is protectively frozen, we are out of touch with our feelings. Releasing the constricted energies in the second chakra will lead to a noticeable increase in vitality and health, due to the improved functioning of the etheric body. The capacity for feeling and intimacy will also be enhanced.

In Tantra, the sacral chakra is related to the water element. Water is often symbolic of the unconscious. When the impersonal forces of the unconscious flow through the psyche, the fragile individuality of the growing ego-self shrinks in fear at confronting these deep and mysterious currents. Unconscious forces push on its tiny island of consciousness with the omnipotence of tidal movements, and sometimes like crashing waves. The tribal and family units create sanctuaries from this vast sea of unconscious forces, while myth and ritual domesticate its power.

In order to establish emotional security, we habitually attempt to control the impersonal forces of the unconscious. Sexual energy, for instance, is often associated with possessiveness and jealousy as we try to own it. On the positive side, the powers of the deep unconscious can be transforming. Sexual energy also includes the potential of transformation experienced through merging with another being and, ultimately, with the transpersonal levels of the psyche.

Health and wholeness on the second chakra level are related to establishing a positive emotional identity. When our past experiences and imprints in the second chakra tell us that we are loved and lovable, and when we accept our feelings and feel that others respect our feelings, then we are able to give and receive emotional support freely. If, on the other hand, our sense of emotional security has been traumatized, we may be unconsciously dominated by either of two general reactions: our awareness of feelings and the ability to receive emotional nurturing from others is inhibited by defense mechanisms, or we are driven by emotional needs that cause us to over-compromise ourselves in order to feed our addiction to approval and support from others.

$\Diamond$

Dealing With
Feelings

Awareness of feelings was the first step that we took out of the instinctual cave of the unconscious. As an evolution of the function of the nervous system, feeling awareness enhanced our sensitivity to the negative and positive influences of the environment. It still acts, consciously or unconsciously, as an underlying motivation for how we respond to our environment.

Although feelings and emotions are closely linked, feelings belong more to the domain of the receptive and impressionable second chakra. Emotions are the expression of our response to feelings, and are related more to the third chakra. To use a simple analogy, imagine a calm lake. When the wind moves across the surface, the lake "feels" it. The impressions of the wind on the water create waves. These waves eventually break on the shore, expressing the force that created them.

In the astral body, stimuli set off ripples of feeling-impressions. A preconscious mechanism judges these feelings to be either pleasure or pain as it filters this information through a series of associations. Chemical, neuromuscular, and perhaps verbal responses are then emoted, if not repressed, onto the shores of consciousness via the etheric and physical bodies.

Feelings have specific meanings, but are often rationalized. Most of us have learned to adjust our feelings to our social mores or to the suppressions of our environments. We have consequently lost touch with our true feelings.

Children are naturally expressive of feelings. How often have we experienced a child sharing some perfectly frank feeling which embarrassed an adult, who then admonished the child? As children we were defenseless against the pain and suppression inflicted by adults and the social structure. Eventually we were forced to protect ourselves by shutting off our awareness. We became lost in our defenses and socially supported roles. The barrier between defensive reality and the world of our real feelings started long ago; it can be quite formidable.

Our defensive egos often judge feelings as problematic, something to be overcome or controlled. Unfortunately, feelings are never done away with once and for all. Painful feelings can happen at any time, they are tolerable only when we learn how to feel and release them in the moment.

Unless feelings are acknowledged and accepted, they cannot be released. Feelings are like streams of water; if there is no resistance, the water flows freely, effortlessly. Resistance creates a dam which turns the free-flowing water either into a stagnant pool, or as the volume and pressure builds, an aggressive and destructive force. It is only our resistance to feelings, and the fear of being rejected for sharing them, that turns their power into a threatening force within us.

The main causes for the separateness and alienation experienced in the second chakra are the defenses and idealism that we escape into to avoid being vulnerable to our feelings. As the second chakra is opened, the ability to feel both pain and pleasure is enhanced. This ambivalent nature of feelings makes it a difficult and courageous task to go beyond the barriers of our defenses back through the history of traumatic memories to regain the feeling self and its capacity for intimacy. This is best accomplished within a supportive environment, either professional or with others doing similar work. Remembering dreams and reviewing the feelings experienced in them is an excellent introduction to the world of feelings within.

$$\diamond$$

Psychic
Sympathy

Psychic sympathy is a phenomenon related to the second chakra which often confuses our feeling experiences. The analogy of a drum head vibrating in sympathy with the vibrations of nearby music is a good way to demonstrate how the astral body, existing in an atmosphere filled with many frequencies of emotional energy, resonates with environmental psychic forces. As these forces interact with the astral body, they—to varying degrees—reproduce similar energy patterns within it.

This is one way to understand how we became programmed by the psychic influences of our earlier environment. As young children just awakening to our own sense of self, we entered the barely conscious realm of the second chakra. Receptive and vulnerable, we went into psychic sympathy with the emotional environment of our parents and culture. Subsequently, vulnerability to various emotional forces on the astral plane is related to patterns that were ingrained in our own emotional bodies. We resonate most readily with external emotional forces that are similar to these ingrained patterns. If, for instance, in the past we had a traumatic experience related to being judged, psychic sympathy may occur when we are judged by another person. We may find ourselves feeling very awkward in the presence of that person. We may even act out the negative projections, behaving in a manner not normal for us, under the influence of these old feelings.

Another aspect of psychic sympathy is associated with tribal psychology. This is a form of collective identification stemming from primitive societies, but still active on the second chakra level of the psyche, when we were unconsciously "at one" with the others in our tribe or clan. Instead of an individual identity, life was lived in and for the group. When we go into psychic sympathy with another person in our lives today, we may still be acting unconsciously from this primitive layer.

Psychic sympathy is often confused with love or caring, but sympathetic reactions are usually based on an unconscious identification with another person. Rather than acting with compassion or empathy, we are responding as if the other person's trauma or problem is happening to us. In these sympathetic responses we may unwisely attempt to assume responsibility for someone else's feelings, or we may act as if the other person's feelings were indeed our own. Or, in a related way, we may be so desperately in need of intimacy that we take on another's feelings in an attempt to feel close.

It is enough to say that we can find ourselves entangled in a variety of confusing emotional states based on the dynamics of psychic sympathy. A willingness to assume responsibility for insecurities and feelings, combined with the tools for self-awareness presented in this book, will provide the reader with the means to mitigate most of the effects of psychic sympathy.

$$\diamond$$

The Inner Mate

As sexual energy (libido or Kundalini) rises up from the first chakra it assumes new connotations. In the second chakra, sexual energy is used in an attempt to overcome the profound sense of aloneness, and a compulsive type of "love" may push us to seek union with another person. Acting from this level of the psyche, we do not share ourselves without ulterior motives! We, albeit unconsciously, use our "beloved" in an attempt to fulfill a deep longing to unite with our "other half." This phantom lover appears as a mysteriously illusive, and incredibly seductive, image of an ideal mate projected from the numinous depths of the psyche.

To gain a better understanding of the dynamics between the conscious self and this inner mate, let's refer once again to Jungian psychology. Although there are basic differences between male and female, we all have masculine and feminine traits within us. Biologically, we contain both male and female genes, the dominant genes accounting for our physiological differences. Psychologically, we have both sexes within, again one or the other being dominant. For the man, the inner woman has been given the name anima (eros, soul) by Carl Jung. The inner man in a woman is called the animus (mind, spirit).

According to Irene Claremont de Castillejo in *Knowing Woman*, a woman's conscious self is attuned to instincts, emotions, and intuitions. Her awareness is generally more diffuse and all-pervading than a man's. She has a tendency to accept or reject things in toto.[2] A woman, therefore, needs to learn how to focus her awareness. The animus helps her clarify her purpose and meaning in life.

When the animus remains unconscious, as it does until a relatively high level of psychological maturity, its qualities cannot be constructively used by a woman. Trapped in the unconscious, he acts in an autonomous way, periodically dominating the woman and causing her to act in a most irritating way. At these times the woman can be unreasonable and argumentative, driving other people up the wall with her irrelevant accusations. Writing on the animus, Jung said, in *Aspects of the Feminine*, that it consists mainly of opinions rather than logically deduced truths.[3]

---

[2]Irene Claremont de Castillejo, *Knowing Woman* (New York: Harper & Row, 1973), p. 77.
[3]Carl Jung, *Aspects of the Feminine* (Princeton, NJ: Princeton University Press, 1982), p. 172.

In contrast to the receptive and life-giving qualities of a woman's basic identity, a man's conscious self is aggressive and driven to develop mastery over the forces of life. His heroic predilections drive him to pursue his conquests—to penetrate the mysteries of Nature. But because his rationalism is focused on objective facts, he needs the woman inside himself (the anima) to fathom the inner realities. She is the muse that inspires him. She reveals his feelings, capacity for relatedness and therefore love, creative imagination, and sense of beauty. Like the man within a woman, the anima is potentially a man's guide to his inner and higher nature, and is the sought after mate that consoles him as he returns home from his exploits.

A man normally represses the woman inside himself because he is uncomfortable with the irrational realm of instinct and emotion. Not getting her due respect, she assails him with mysterious moods and vain indulgences. An anima controlled man can be just as bitchy and temperamental as any woman. Or, such a man can be hopelessly dominated by the woman upon whom he projects his negative anima.

Although the anima and animus are archetypes, as individuals we have a personal interpretation of their particular characteristics. The animus is founded on "Father," and includes the totality of patriarchal values. The anima is grounded in "Mother," with unconscious memories of matriarchal times. In addition to our personal experiences of these two primary sources, all manner of social values and our impressions of the opposite sex (including past life influences) are responsible for our individual renderings of the inner woman and inner man.

The anima and animus act as catalysts for relationship when projected mutually onto persons of the opposite sex. Through the path of relationships, these inner guides potentially lead us to the wholeness we are seeking within ourselves. The lovesickness that marks the beginning of romantic relationships is caused by the numinous charge of the anima and animus. In addition to being turned on by this upsurgence of sexual-romantic feelings, we also feel uplifted by the idealized qualities projected onto us by our new lover. We enjoy believing these things about ourselves until it becomes apparent that the other person is not in love with us, but with the fantasy that we are expected to fulfill. When the projection screen upon which we have projected our ideal mates becomes torn by the wear and tear of day-to-day relating, we see through it to the other person. We may then feel hurt and cheated, it is then that we should look inward to the other in ourselves.

Our inner mates have their own negative traits. Their ill tempers can destroy our ability to have meaningful relationships. For example, a woman may experience a long series of relationships confirming her conviction that men are out to dominate her, rather than understanding that her real conflict is with the negative and domineering aspects of her own masculinity. She will continue fighting and blaming the men in her life for her sense of oppression and worthlessness. She will consequently be driven to undermine and devalue men as she struggles to bolster her self-esteem and sense of personal power. The hostility generated by possession of a negative animus is quite different from the strength and clarity of a woman who has integrated her masculine side.

When a man is possessed by his negative feminine side he may become melancholic, vain, or nit-picky, etc. He may project the cause of these feelings onto a woman, blaming her for making him feel this way. When identified with the negative woman within himself, he may feel helpless and unable to confront the hardships in life. In order to attain his ambitions he may feel he has to resort to manipulation or trickery.

The anger and resentment a man feels as a result of being let down by the woman upon whom he has bestowed the idealized projection of his anima is a cruel blow. Similarly, if a woman does not take the responsibility to befriend her own masculine side, she will always be able to find some weakness, fear, or imperfection in a man to destroy her fantasy of him as a hero who should be fulfilling all her demands and expectations. The mistrust and hopelessness generated from these experiences are a poor foundation for future relationships and the task of psychological growth.

There are four beings involved in a romantic relationship, two people and their inner counterparts. It is best to relate to these unconscious partners with the respect they deserve, for the more unconscious they remain, the more autonomous and potent they become. We cannot repress or control them without unfortunate consequences.

Dreams offer great insight into the nature of the inner partner. We can learn a great deal by paying particular attention to the characters of the opposite sex and our relationship to them in our dreams. Keeping a diary in which we record anima or animus dreams is a good way to get to know our inner mates. Reflection upon the main themes in past romantic relationships will also reveal various facets of our contrasexual nature.

There is a profound symbolic meaning contained in the images projected onto the object of our sexual desire. Integrating the unconscious contents embodied in these images is an important step in our personal growth.

$$\Diamond$$

Tantric
Sexuality

What do you think about during sex? What are you feeling? What's happening in your body? Why do you do it? The difference between normal sexuality and Tantric sex lies in the answers to these questions.

Average sexual relations are, for the most part, based on physical passion and romantic emotions. Our addiction to sensual excitement, romance, and the sense of emotional security experienced in these relations, often subjects us to a variety of unpleasant results. In addition, much of our vital energy can be dissipated in careless, if not admittedly neurotic, and unconsciously driven indulgences.

Through the skillful means of Tantra, we can guide these powerful libidinous and romantic forces to more subtle and rewarding realms of expression. Through Tantric sexuality we learn how to withdraw our personal attachments from the powerful forces at play between a man and a woman. For a man, his consort is no longer his mate, but the Goddess—embodiment of the wisdom-insight of the Englightened Mind. For a woman, her consort is the Deity—embodiment of the skillful means to Enlightenment. The various impersonal forces symbolized in the Tantric deities activate, and allow us to worship, the unconscious aspects of our contrasexual self.

In a traditional setting, there are four main stages in this process. The first is for those of us (who are not nuns or monks) still controlled by romantic desires. We are free to have sexual relations with others who are unskilled in Tantra at this stage as long as we identify ourselves and our partners as deities filled with compassion.

The next stage is for those of us who have remaining attachments, but who have acquired more appreciation of the task of spiritual unfoldment. It is important now that we practice sexual yoga only with a person who is at the same level of understanding. If we are studying with a lama, he may chose a consort who is more skilled or advanced in Tantric practice. In this context, we begin to employ the various breath, muscular, and visual techniques of sexual yoga to open certain psychic channels and stimu-late the Kundalini energy.

At the third stage, meditations with deities in sexual embrace are practiced. This leads ultimately to the fourth stage where the need for reverential objects is transcended.

In normal lovemaking, the breath, heartbeat, mind, and sex glands are excited—all of which race toward orgasm. In Tantric sex, one learns how to articulate these functions; rather than being dissipated, biopsychic energies are allowed to build and resonate throughout the body-mind.

A slow and full breath is used to remain grounded and alert during sexual meditation. Harmonizing the breath with the partner—one breathing in while the other breathes out—creates a psychic energy link and establishes a tranquil rhythm.

The male also uses methods to refrain from orgasm. Aside from the obvious extension of the duration of love-making through the retention of ejaculation by the male, there are vital and biological benefits. Semen is a very concentrated nutrient, containing hormones, minerals, and amino acids. It is said that one ejaculation is equal in nutritional value to two wholesome meals. Hence, an ill or weak man should guard against orgasm, and a healthy man should be careful not to deplete his store of vital nutrients.

Although a woman's sexual secretions also contain potent nutrients, their loss is not as extreme as for a man. Hence, her need to restrain from orgasm does not have the same biological import; indeed, female orgasm is encouraged in both Tantric and Taoist sexual rituals. Her feminine essence is considered to have a vitalizing effect on the lovemaking, nurturing the circulation of psychic energies through the conjoined subtle bodies of both practitioners. In theory, her essence is inexhaustible and nour-ishes the male energy which is easily depleted.

Sexual stimulation releases hormones that are reportedly very beneficial for the entire organism. Ancient yogis discovered that they could recirculate vital energy and these precious nutrients throughout the body-mind with techniques used in sexual yoga.

In normal sexual activity, the emissions of the prostrate gland and seminal vesicles are expelled during ejaculation. In *Sexual Energy Ecstasy*, the authors claim that with methods which prevent ejaculation, these secretions are contained in the urethra and slowly absorbed into the lymph system to be recirculated throughout the body.[4]

They also add a word of caution: techniques for blocking the natural expulsion of semen after the contraction of the sex glands, tensing rectal muscles or thrusting one's finger into the perineum below the root of the penis, may cause sexual fluids to back up into the bladder and prevent the prostrate gland from emptying itself. As a frequent practice, this can cause congestion, and hence, disease in these organs. For the same reasons, a man who is highly sexed may find it unhealthy to repress these secretions on a regular basis.[5]

The ancient Chinese, while encouraging a man to have sex as often as possible, warned against ejaculation in the winter months, but considered it all right during the spring when the tide of sexual energy waxes high. In our own personal energy cycles, it may not be harmful, but indeed healthy, to release sexual fluids during periods of excess energy.

In general, it is advisable for the male to remain calm and guard against passing the "point of no return," the point when the sex glands begin to spasm. This allows the sexual fluids to seep out gradually and be absorbed. The secret here is to concentrate on your identification with the deity and its state of meditative awareness (which enhances as you awake the Kundalini force and

---

[4]David Alan Ramsdale and Ellen Jo Dorfman, *Sexual Energy Ecstasy* (Playa Del Ray, CA: Peak Skill, 1985), p. 197.
[5]Ramsdale and Dorfman, *Sexual Energy Ecstasy*, p. 198.

enter into deeper levels of appreciation of the states of consciousness symbolized by the deities) while allowing the female to assume the active sexual role.

The vital energy used in sexual activities is also a concern in Tantra. The amount of energy that can be aroused through sexual means can best be demonstrated by remembering a time when you went to bed so tired that you were collapsing. If you then became sexually stimulated, your weary condition may suddenly have changed. As sexual energy began to flow through you, you became invigorated with a vitality that sustained you throughout the period of love-making. This vital force is considered by the Tantric yogi to be very precious.

There is a very powerful connection between the mind and the vital energies stimulated by sex. For example, one day while I was meditating, I had a very graphic experience of the concrete relationship between the two. My mind started wandering and found its way to contemplate the physical beauty of a woman that I had recently met. One thing led to another and I suddenly realized that I was sitting there in meditation with an erection. My mind had directed my vital energies right down into the sexual organ. In a similar manner, the vital forces usually squandered in sexual activities can be directed to circulate into higher functions of the psyche. Such use of the sexual forces also has a very healing effect on the body, circulating vitality throughout the bio-psychic organism in a manner similar to that of Acupuncture or Polarity Therapy.

Entering the median nerve at the Navel Center, from the sexual region, the vital force moves through the middle of other nerve centers. Becoming the Fire force of Wisdom-energy, it rises upward and pervades all the nerve channels, untying all psychic "knots" . . . . (Six Doctrines of Naropa)[6]

Tantric sexual rituals use many symbols and procedures to create a sense of sacredness. The sexual rite is also performed at an auspicious time. One such time is the new moon. The conjunction of the sun and moon in the heavens is considered to be an appropriate time to honor the harmonization of the solar and lunar forces within the body-mind.

For people who have a great deal of experience in meditation, there may be no need for a pre-arranged ritual. Mutual sensitivity and an intuitive appreciation for the organic unfoldment of subtle energies may serve as a guide. For others, a ritual bath, anointing with scented oils, candle or fire light, meditative music, and an agreed-upon series of visualizations and breathing techniques all help create the appropriate circumstances for union. To start this practice, I suggest a simple sexual technique:

Begin with the woman lying on her back, and the man lying on his left side, to the right of her. After harmonizing your breath with one another, the woman raises her legs, bringing her knees to her chest. This allows the man to gently penetrate her. She then lets her legs down and intertwines them with her mate.

While continuing to breathe together, feel the heat of the sexual union rising up the spine with each inhale. With each exhale feel the milk-white nectar in the head center, melted by the sexual fire, running down into all of the chakras. Spend time feeling the bliss created by this nectar as it saturates and pours out into the subtle nerve currents of each chakra.

The woman will want to learn how to contract and strengthen the muscles of her vagina. By contracting these muscles around the man's penis, which is deep within her, great pleasure is generated. Her rhythmical contractions ought to be

---

[6]Nik Douglas and Penny Slinger, *Sexual Secrets* (Rochester, VT: Destiny Books, 1979), p. 300. You can find this material elsewhere, as the Six Doctrines of Naropa is an old text, but readers may find this particular reference helpful.

enough for the man to maintain an erection, and thus all other movement is kept to a minimum. She may begin by isolating those muscles while urinating; the muscles that allow her to stop the flow of her urine are the same muscles she will need to develop. By inserting a finger, or other suitable object, into the vagina and closing down on it, she can learn to articulate and strengthen these muscles.

The man may also contract the muscles that cause his penis to swell and move slightly within her yoni. Each partner may contract during their respective inhalations, imagining that they are sucking the sexual fire from the place of union up the spine.

After about a half an hour of this Tantric embrace, it is possible to feel waves of energy that may cause spontaneous contractions and pleasurable sensations throughout the body. Relax and enjoy them, open your body to bliss.

◇

Consort Meditation

The following meditation is not traditional, but it is one that I find very helpful for contacting and integrating the anima and animus. It is also useful for developing the passive alertness required for more advanced levels of meditation.

Begin by settling into an inner calmness. Next allow an image of a person of the opposite sex to appear in your mind's eye. Be careful not to permit the rational mind to interfere as you focus your undivided attention on every detail, movement, and feeling associated with the various activities and transformations of this inner mate.

The experiences that you have during this meditation may include the whole spectrum of possible expression of the contra-sexual side of your self. By simply witnessing these, you will be introduced to the many facets of your inner mate. Surrender completely to the god or goddess in whatever form he or she manifests to you.

At the end of the meditation, if the episodes do not contain a sexual experience, you can choose one of the forms in which the god or goddess appears to you and imagine in detail a Tantric sexual experience. Once again, allow yourself to be guided in this by your consort. The feeling of completeness and love that are generated in this meditation can be carried over into everyday life by imagining (and acting as if) your consort accompanies you throughout the day. When you go to bed at night, you can imagine that your consort is there beside you. Fall asleep feeling the love that you share. In the morning, begin the day by greeting your consort, etc. When you learn some of the other meditations in this book, you might want to imagine that your consort transforms into the various deities used in them.

After this initial meditation, you may want to choose specific times to perform the consort meditation. The new or full moon, or at all four phases of the moon are good suggestions. It is also a good idea to begin keeping a journal of the more profound experiences that you'll be having in meditation.

CHAPTER
FOUR

♦

THE KINGDOM
OF JEWEL-LIKE
RADIANCE

*T*he third chakra is related to the fire element in Hindu Tantra, and its Sanskrit name, *Manipura*, means "shining like a jewel." It has ten petals, "the color of heavy-laden rain clouds." Within the lotus is the Agni mandala, a red inverted triangle that symbolizes the fire element. Inside of it is a ram, demonstrating the obnoxious qualities of the rational mind driven by desire. (See fig. 12 on page 80.)

The third chakra is the second story of the Buddhist sacred temple. Because the Buddhists combine the first and second chakras, the element of water is related to the third chakra. The water element is symbolized with a white circle. Lama Govinda, in *Foundations of Tibetan Mysticism*, points out that the assimilating qualities of the water element are related to the assimilating aspects of the third chakra through the idea that it transforms gross elements into psychic factors and absorbs unconscious contents and immaterial forces.[1]

---

[1]Lama Govinda, *Foundations of Tibetan Mysticism* (York Beach, ME: Samuel Weiser, 1974; and London: Rider & Co., 1974), p. 179.

The Primordial Buddha Ratnasambhava, embodiment of the psychic function of feeling judgment, sits on the throne in the third chakra. (See fig. 13 on page 82.) Though he is normally associated with the earth element and the color yellow, his Wisdom of Equality can transform our self-centered feeling judgments into a universal feeling identity based on the inner unity of all things. Hence through a profound emotional experience of egolessness, we can develop analytical perception and discriminative wisdom without sacrificing our connection to the Great Unity. Ratnasambhava's obscuring passions are pride and egotism.

Located in the solar plexus, the third chakra provides vital energy to the pancreas and liver, which govern the assimilation and metabolism of energy derived from food. Aside from the fire of digestion, the third chakra is also animated by the fire of desire and the power of emotions. Hence, during the process of clearing

Figure 12. The third chakra, Manipura. Within the lotus of ten petals, we find the Agni mandala, an inverted red triangle. The seed mantra RAM invokes the god of sacrificial fire, Agni. Agni's vehicle is a ram.

and opening the third chakra, digestive problems may coincide with dramatic periods of emotional instability as repressed emotions are released. Power trips and ego trips are products of a fired-up, but undeveloped or defensive third chakra. A healthy sense of self-esteem and personal power mark a successfully awakened third chakra.

The third chakra is also associated with the mythological stage of the hero and development of the ego-consciousness. As a center of consciousness, the ego becomes an integrative force strong enough to take diffuse elements from the inner and outer worlds and digest them into a sense of identity. As the ego stabilizes, its ability to assimilate the contents of the unconscious mind increases, and more psychic energy becomes available to it. The ego transforms this energy into power to control its individual world, make conscious choices, and resist the demands of the unconscious. Thus, the ego gains a certain volition over the instinctual life of body and emotion and an ability to manipulate its external environment.

As a center of power, the third chakra regulates the flow of vital energies through the body. When this chakra is blocked, either chronically or temporarily, due to a power struggle, we feel physically lethargic and may also feel depressed and irritable. By becoming aware of the psychic energies at war in the third chakra, overcoming our fear of conflict, and taking command, we can reclaim our power. These symptoms vanish and a distinct sense of empowerment is likely to prevail as the free flow of psychic energy through the third chakra activates the mythological archetypes of the hero.

The opening of the third chakra may also result in the development of certain ESP and clairvoyant abilities. We may leave the physical body and have conscious experience in the astral world, and dreams are also more easily recalled. However, psychic information received through these avenues of perception may be

Figure 13. Ratnasambhava is the lord of the third chakra and embodies the Wisdom of Equality. His color is yellow and he rules the Earth Element. His right hand reaches down, with palm turned outward, in the Vara Mudra, signifying charity. His left hand holds a magic jewel. Illustration is Plate 2 from *Foundations of Tibetan Mysticism*, by Lama Govinda (published in 1974 by Samuel Weiser, York Beach, Maine, and Rider & Co., London) and is reproduced by permission of the publishers.

confused with subjective desires from within the astral body, and thus they are not always reliable sources of guidance.

In the third chakra we find the desire or impulse to sprout forth from the depths of the unconscious and collective influences in a pioneering attempt to discover our own identity. This individualistic aspect of the third chakra may prove to be a source of insecurity when it does, in fact, separate us from others and from old familiar patterns. Another danger with this Mars-like use of the will is that it is naturally colored with self-centered desire and acted out in a "headstrong" (like a ram) manner.

Self-expression can be used positively to channel emotions and serve as a vehicle of self-discovery, or it can lead to a megalomania as we attempt to validate our sense of self. The power we receive from others, in the form of attention or adulation, is used to boost self-esteem. Sexual relations, when based on this aspect of the third chakra, can be seen as a performance and an ego trip. Characteristics like arrogance, pompousness, and displays of melodrama are also associated with it. On the other hand, charm, warmth, generosity, and a sunny disposition may radiate from the more magnanimous aspects of the third chakra.

If we do not bring the issues relating to the psychological functions of the third chakra into consciousness and resolve them, our relations with others is experienced on the basis of submission versus domination. We view others not as peers, but as inferior or superior. Alfred Adler, who coined the term inferiority complex, founded a school of psychology that focused on this aspect of the third chakra.

Adler observed many of his clients being preoccupied with issues of self-esteem, adequacy, competition, and domination; he even realized that the sex act can be experienced in these terms. Adler targeted childhood feelings of inadequacy and inferiority as the source of our need to develop compensatory attitudes of superiority. This is undoubtedly true, but in my experience, regardless of age, these tendencies seem to run rampant here in the kingdom of the jewel-like radiance.

$$\Diamond$$

The Shadow and Persona

The *shadow* is a Jungian term for the parts of the psyche that are suppressed by the ego. In growing up, we hid many aspects of ourselves from others in order to be loved and accepted. The hidden shadow remains immature, but has an innate desire for conscious recognition and approval. Another aspect of the shadow can be related to past lives, in which we acted out some of the negative or socially unacceptable characteristics of ourselves. Unfortunately the shadow, like the hideous person in horror movies who has been locked up in an attic all its life, often terrifies us; we'd prefer to keep it locked up and forget about it.

Because it is unconscious, the shadow is most commonly experienced as a projection onto another person, usually a person of the same sex. The characteristics that we react to in a person we dislike are good reflections of the part of ourselves we despise. A second outlet for the shadow is in dreams, where we are hunted or attacked by animals, or a hostile or repulsive member of the same sex. A third manifestation is reacting emotionally to a degree inappropriate for a given situation.

Attempts to cover up the shadow with socially acceptable ego behavior is useless. In order to make peace with the shadow, it is necessary to cease judging and repressing it. The ego will eventually need to embrace all the child-like resentments, needs, aggressions, insecurities, will to power, and desires contained in the shadow. If it does not, large quantities of psychic energy will remain trapped in conflicting subpersonalities that embody these repressed contents. The more these are suppressed, the more freedom the subpersonalities have to vandalize the life of the conscious self. In extreme cases, persistent denial of the negative side of the shadow results in what is clinically called a psycho-pathological complex.

It is not until we are shocked into seeing ourselves as we really are, instead of how we wish or assume we are, that the journey toward our essential individuality can begin. Facing the shadow requires humility. Trust is also a concern here. If we can trust that the shadow will not destroy our lives if we let it out, we can more easily begin integrating it instead of continuing to project it on to others.

The shadow may also contain positive qualities that have remained undeveloped because the self-image is overly modest or shy. There may have been no support or frame of reference in our early environment for some of these potential qualities to develop.

A look at mythology will demonstrate several variations on the potential function of the shadow. In myth, the shadow is often dramatized as an animal or curious companion that saves the hero from an untimely end through its instincts. In other cases, we find the hero combating a brutal enemy whose intended malice enigmatically provides just what the hero needs. These mythic themes illustrate how the shadow actually contains missing elements that are valuable to the ego.

While the shadow is the aspect of ourselves damned to the unconscious, the *persona* is the mask the ego wears to present itself to the outer world. In dreams, for example, the persona may be represented by a disguise or costume. As children we created or adopted images that attained for us cultural and parental acceptance. The persona, therefore, reflects the ego's identification with parental and societal standards.

The persona can also be thought of as the ego trips used to justify our existence. Growing up, many of us experienced some kind of emotional deprivation and thus did not forge a strong sense of self-esteem. As adults, we keep this basic insecurity hidden. The defense mechanisms adopted to deal with both emotional pain and an unjustified existence are some of the desperate hands that shape the masks we wear. Unfortunately, this defensive posture of the ego hardens us and we act in ways that are not always conducive to the satisfaction of our needs.

As children, many of us learned quickly that it was useless to ask directly for what we wanted; we instead decided to stop expressing our feelings and needs, resorted to acting out our anger, or became manipulative. As adults, therefore, we have a history of unfulfilled emotional needs and desires that are carried into our relations with others. Without communicating clearly, we often project a host of expectations and demands onto relationships, only to feel again and again the pain and confusion from the past. Consumed by anger and pain when our expectations are not met, we rely on psychological defense mechanisms to contain ourselves. Frequently we make requests as if we expect to be denied, which either further inhibits us, or causes us to be overly demanding. These, of course, are not the most positive or effective ways to get the desired result.

As we disconnect our sense of identity from the power to obtain what we want from others, we can learn that we have a responsibility to ourselves at least to acknowledge, if not express, feelings and desires. It is more important to express ourselves honestly and directly than it is to affect and manipulate others. Through expression, we dissipate the emotional charge and can learn to direct it in the most positive way. By sharing what is felt rather than making a demand, we find it much easier to let go and not be dominated by our own reactions and defenses. Through acting like benevolent and wise parents in regard to our desires and emotions, we can lovingly listen to them and firmly guide them, rather than fight or suppress them.

Another ramification of the dynamics between the shadow and persona is the judgments we make on others. In an effort to defend our sense of self-worth—our bright and shiny masks—we often find fault with others before they can see our shadow. We all need to feel good about ourselves. If we do not feel accepted and recognized, we turn bitter and cynical. We become jealous of others and may go through life focused on pointing out all the ways others don't deserve to receive what we feel we are being deprived of.

In the same way that social convention can trap us in a rigid order, part of our strict self image (persona) can dominate our creativity and individuality. In Transactional Analysis, this aspect is named the punitive parent because it is the part of us that became just like mom and dad. It is always telling us what we should and shouldn't do, and punishing us when we don't obey. Through a psychological revolution, the child within can be freed to explore and develop.

The shadow has an inverse relationship to the energy invested in the persona. An overdeveloped persona pushes the shadow deeper into the unconscious where it becomes more dangerous. Horrifying crimes committed in the name of the state or church are examples of an overdeveloped persona. At the other end of the spectrum, an underdeveloped persona makes it difficult to function in the social world. We automatically alienate ourselves if we are unable to accept any of the roles and rules of society. At either extreme, we are inhibited in realizing and manifesting our individuality.

When consciously expressed, both the shadow and the persona are essential implements for self-discovery and operation in the world. One important task of the ego-self at this stage of development, then, is to integrate the qualities of the shadow and the persona, while not identifying with them.

◇

Sex, Love, and
Power

Since self-esteem and a sense of personal power are directly connected to feeling loved and accepted, most people depend on others to make them feel worthwhile. When the need is great, we compromise ourselves to get love and acceptance. Though this seems to work for a while, it is almost sure to breed resentment in the long run. The greater the need, and the greater the power we give to the person who supplies that need, the more subservient and powerless we feel.

The need for self-esteem and a sense of adequacy need to be fulfilled. Instead of power games, this may mean digging deep into parental and cultural indoctrination. For instance, we could begin with looking at the initial programming regarding sexual identity. Overcoming the deep sense of guilt and shame we may have experienced in the conflict between our awakening sexual desire and our particular social and sexual taboos is obviously important. Was sex something nasty? Many of us grew up with the attitude that, for some mysterious reason, our sexual identity was something we felt ashamed of and had to hide.

In an even more limiting way, there may be insidious sexual-emotional bonds, usually with the parent of the opposite sex. Parents may never have given us permission for the expression of our sexual identity. A mother may unconsciously not want to let go of her son by covertly preventing another woman from taking him away from her. A father may covet his daughter, suppressing his own strong feelings of sexual love for her by jealously holding on to her and inhibiting her maturation.

By liberating ourselves from these limitations, we can be free to express the full power of sexuality in a positive way. It feels good to celebrate the vitality of life through sexual relations. Good loving promotes a certain kind of self-esteem that enables us to feel and express love even more fully.

Another important factor to consider is the education of the ego in regard to its relationship to the impersonal force of love. The ego's power is a double-edged sword; we need to wield it skillfully. On one hand we are indebted to life to carve out an individual and conscious identity from the prima materia of the collective unconscious. Ironically, once we have a well-defined sense of self we are obliged to sacrifice it and its claims to power in order to enter a higher order of conscious existence. Not only do we live by the sword, if we do not give it up at the appropriate time, it turns against us.

Love and power are antagonistic, an abundance of one diminishes the other. The ego's power, its desire to control and possess, precludes the openness and surrender that love requires. Love is universal – divine – yet the ego wants to own it, to have it when, how, and with whom it so desires. But when the ego brandishes its sword to conquer love, it is always frustrated. Until it sacrifices its will to power, the ego cannot enter the mystery that love is, and continue its journey to the more sublime realms of consciousness.

$$\Diamond$$

Emotions and the Astral World

The feeling responses that we studied in the second chakra are expressed as emotions. Emotional charges manifest themselves from the astral body, via the chakras, to the main nerve ganglia and endocrine glands, affecting hormonal secretions, changes in circulation rate, blood pressure, respiration, blood sugar, and neuromuscular excitation. In a primitive person, emotions are expressed instantaneously. With further evolution of the nervous system, the instinctive emotional reflex is delayed and can be changed by conscious intervention. This means we have some volition over the unconscious drives of the body, and some distance and control over the irrational effects of emotions.

In metaphysical teachings, the world of emotions is often referred to as the astral plane. The Tantric view of the universe also shows us a number of dimensions existing at different frequencies. Just as various frequencies in the electromagnetic spectrum can simultaneously exist in the same place without interfering with one another, so can the physical and the astral worlds. We are rarely directly aware of the astral realm, although it is the place where we go in our dreams, and its energy manifests itself in our lives as emotions. In his book, *Journeys Out of the Body*, based on twelve years of astral projection, Robert Monroe lucidly describes the astral plane as a reality made up of the desires and fears that are normally repressed in our physical lives. For instance, he relates how his fears were more powerful than his sexual desires, which in themselves were "tremendous obstacles." He goes on to explain how until he was able to discipline these raw emotions, he was doomed to wander in the more unpleasant areas of the astral world populated by "disjoined personalities" and other "animate beings."[2]

Out-of-body experiences, either in the dream state or other altered states of consciousness, show us that emotions and desires have a life of their own in the astral body, above and beyond connection with the physical organism.

------

[2]Robert A. Monroe, *Journeys Out of the Body* (New York: Doubleday, 1971), pp. 77–78.

Though we all have an astral body, the level of its development and our ability to use it differs greatly. There are relatively few people who can consciously use the astral body as an independent vehicle, separate from the physical. Although we are sometimes conscious on the astral plane while dreaming, most people do not retain this awareness upon awakening. The level of astral consciousness is foreign to the physically oriented rational mind. Because young children have not yet learned to create a distinct separation between their inner and outer worlds, they are more likely to remember their astral experiences. There are times, however, when we may awaken with the peculiar feeling of having experienced an unusually vivid dream. These are called lucid dreams and are marked by an uncanny sense of being "awake" in the dream. We will explore lucid dreams more in chapter 6.

Astral means star-like, the luminous qualities of the emotional body inspired the name astral. The iridescent hues clairvoyantly perceived in the aura of a person through whom spiritual love and wisdom radiate are truly a beauty to behold. The surface of the astral body resembles the vapors of dry ice, the luminous mists seem to swirl, rise, and sink back again. Specific emotions seem to move in portions of the astral body that relate to the appropriate areas of the body and to the chakras. Primitive emotions related to the survival of the body tend to gravitate to the bottom of the aura, below the first chakra. Sexual feelings, jealousy, and emotional insecurity consolidate near the second chakra. Anger and arrogance gather near the third chakra, love or grief around the fourth, and so on. Sudden or powerful emotions may temporarily overcome the entire astral body. As this passes, the normal vibrational rate and color patterns return.

Gravitating around its particular characteristic patterns, the astral body shifts and changes into the variety of emotional states we experience. It is also greatly affected by physical habits and mental attitudes. Living in unclean conditions, subjecting the physical body to alcohol, drugs, certain kinds of music, cigarette smoke, pollution, and large quantities of animal foods will adversely affect the astral body due to the astral counterparts of these things.

The astral body is particularly susceptible to impressions from the mind. Shapes within the astral matter can be clairvoyantly seen to emerge and dissolve in response to currents of thoughts. Strong thoughts may create astral forms that seem to acquire a life of their own. These forms may project into the astral world, populating the adjacent environment and affecting other people. Negative thoughts can create astral monsters which have the power to devour the joy and love in our lives. Confronting and befriending them can be a Herculean task.

In addition to integrating the shadow, learning how to express feelings, and communicating clearly our desires, several things can be done to transform and raise the level of vibration in the astral body. The physical body can be purified and exorcised. Eating wholesome and non-toxic food develops their counterparts in the astral body. Exercise and sports are effective expressions for dammed up emotional energy.

Enthusiasm and exhilaration have a cleansing and uplifting effect on the astral body. Surfing, skiing, sailing, horseback riding, and a hot game of tennis or soccer generate a sense of aliveness and excitement which offers an alternative to negative emotional patterns and an opportunity to develop a store of positive emotional experiences. Playing a musical instrument or singing offers both cathartic outlets and avenues of creative expression for the emotions. Creative endeavors, such as dancing, sewing, or art, encourage emotional expression and generate feelings of satisfaction and accomplishment. Listening to inspirational music and walking in the grandeur of nature are also very purifying and uplifting to the astral body. A keen awareness of habitual thought processes will also give an opportunity to reform the mental forces influencing the astral body.

From a Tantric perspective, merely acting out emotions is often, like repressing them, a way of attempting to get rid of them. Transmuting emotions into their related Wisdom Energy happens first by accepting them as they are, by not wanting to change them or trying to get rid of them. In order to do this we need to learn how to refrain from judging emotions as good or bad and experience them in their suchness. Disassociating them from the ego's point of reference, we can be aware of their raw energy. In *Cutting Through Spiritual Materialism*, Chogyam Trungpa compares transmuting emotions to subjugation of demons by the great yogi Milarepa. When Milarepa was meditating in his cave he was confronted by a throng of demons. No matter how he tried to get rid of them, they continued to haunt him until he stopped relating to them as something bad. When he began accepting their presence, they transformed into dakinis, feminine spirits who represent the generic energies of life.[3]

The Laws of Karma

All thoughts, emotions, and actions generate patterns of energy in the body-mind. These patterns are like seeds. They will produce either good or bad fruit, depending on the nature of the original impetus. The Eastern teachings about karma (a Sanskrit word meaning action) suggest that all present life conditions have been determined by past actions. In the same way, future circumstances are created by present actions. At a meditation retreat,

[3]Chogyam Trungpa, *Cutting Through Spiritual Materialism* (Boston: Shambhala, 1973), p. 241.

teacher Goenka shared this old Buddhist story to dem-
ow karma works:

day a wealthy merchant came to Buddha and
offered him a large sum of money to carry out a ritual for
his dead father. Brahmin priests customarily performed
this ritual for a deceased person to release the soul from
all its negative karma. Knowing this to be a futile
endeavor, Buddha was reluctant to accept this request.
However, he saw that the man was very sincere and
replied that if the merchant was willing to assist him, he
would perform the ceremony. Buddha told the man to
place several white stones and some ghee (clarified butter) into a ceramic jar and place it in the river. He then
instructed him to break the jar with a stick. The merchant followed these directives and returned the next
day. Buddha asked him what happened when he broke
the jar. The merchant reported that the stones sank to
the bottom and the ghee floated to the surface. Buddha
then pointed out that the laws of karma are just like the
natural laws that caused the stones to sink and the ghee
to float. He told the merchant that the weight of his
father's karma will cause him to gravitate to certain situations in his next life regardless of any ceremony that he
(Buddha) might perform.

The concept of karma is inseparable from the sense of individual
identity. The creation of karma depends on a self who performs
actions. As the combination of all past experiences, emotions,
and thoughts which have uniquely structured our psyches, karma
is the very stuff and glue of our individual identities. We do not
have karma, we *are* it!

Karma is the force that compels the soul to incarnate life after
life. It is the thread of continuity that weaves through the complex texture of patterns generated and regenerated by our actions

and reactions, lifetime after lifetime. Throughout history we have often loved and hated the same people. We are literally reliving the same old romances and feuds. If not with the same people, at least with similar ones that we attract to us because of our karmic predispositions.

Karma is not fate. In each life we have opportunities to let go of attachments and aversions, to heal all the hurts and animosities and change the causative patterns in the psyche. Though we reap what is sown, we have the freedom to sow new and better seeds that will bear different fruit.

Unlike the Christian tradition, which teaches us to pray to a Supreme Being to save us from our sins, in Tantra our redemption lies in our own hands. In fact, there is no concept of sin in Buddhism; there is only folly based on ignorance. Wisdom brings insight regarding the effects of our actions, hence we are less likely to perform evil deeds. If we do, we are damning ourselves. It is not the Supreme Being who is punishing us, or an outside evil force that is leading us astray; it is ourselves. This is a much healthier perspective, one which empowers us.

The Buddhists maintain that there are ten ways of creating negative karma: three associated with the body, four with speech, and three with the mind. The bodily actions include: killing or inflicting physical harm, stealing or taking that which has not been freely given, and sexual misconduct (sexual behavior that is inappropriate for either party). Those of speech are: lying, slander, foul language, and gossip. The negative actions of the mind are: having ill will toward others or ourself, being jealous of the possessions or characteristics of others, and maintaining incorrect views about oneself and the nature of reality. In short, whatever harms another person or ourselves produces negative karma.

On the other hand, good karma is created by actions that truly benefit ourselves and others. The fruits of these actions are termed "merit." Like negative karma, the effects of merit are long-lasting. The Buddhists, therefore, encourage the collection of merit to offset the results of negative karma. Hindu teachings, on the other hand, emphasize non-attachment to the fruits of our actions. Performing meritorious actions only to ward off the threat of bad karma may reinforce the manipulative and self-centered aspects of the ego.

Average people are caught in a thick web of karma from past lives. To work through these karmic patterns will take many lifetimes. An attitude of acceptance helps tremendously. With the belief that whatever befalls us is the direct manifestation of past actions, energy is not wasted fighting and resenting others (or life itself) for what has been self-created. This acceptance helps us concentrate on doing things that are more favorable for our health and welfare.

The cause and effect functions of karma don't necessarily conform to ideas of linear or chronological time. The fruits of karma ripen only under the appropriate conditions. As we progress in our spiritual work (perhaps proud of our collected merit), we may confront karmic situations from many different periods in the life of our souls. The timing of the fruition of these karmas is based on many variables: groups of certain souls incarnating together, certain social conditions and collective karmas, the level of our spiritual understanding, and so on. Therefore, no matter how far along the spiritual path we may seem to be, we need to be ever ready to accept and work through old karma.

The Buddhists speak of three poisons of the mind: ignorance (the ego-centered perspective), anger (including all forms of aversion), and lust (all manner of desires). These three poisons are considered to be the root cause of all negative karma. Refusing to yield to desires and harmful actions that create negative karma is the best way of preventing it, but that is not always possible or safe. Repressing these poisons without uprooting their sources deep within the psyche may cause severe disturbances in the body-mind. For example, John Blofeld, in *Tantric Mysticism of Tibet*, relates how some monks, who would rather die than break their vows of celibacy, have developed significant nervous disorders.[4] Our own Christian Church also has its share of neurotic clergy who have either turned to drink or acts of perversion. It is wiser to yield to desires while remaining attentive to the act, the underlying motivation provoking it, and its consequences. With insight, the underlying purpose of the behavior can often be integrated, dissipating the compulsion.

When we lose belief in ourselves as separate units of consciousness, we discover that there really is no doer, no individual will, and thus no creation of karma. It is to this end that the teachings about karma are ultimately directed in the Tantric tradition.

Insight
Meditation

Concentration can be considered a simple act of resting the awareness on an object while letting go of everything else. In deep meditation, this letting go eventually extends to the breath and the body, causing an overall slowing down of its metabolism. Indeed, the spontaneous slowing of the rate of breathing is a good gauge for the depth of meditation. This calming of the mind and physiological functions promotes trance-states called *jhanas*. These states are an important step, but not the goal, of meditation. In fact, these trance-states may prove to be an obstacle to further progress because, even though we can block mental activity, our awareness may become dull. In a lecture in New York, Kalu Rinpoche warned, "at worst, tranquility meditation is like an

---

[4]John Blofeld, *Tantric Mysticism of Tibet* (New York: E. P. Dutton, 1970), p. 80.

animal in hibernation." Ideally, tranquility meditation is like a "smooth highway on which we drive to arrive at more advanced levels of Tantric meditation."

The next step in Buddhist meditation is a heightening of the clarity and sensitivity of consciousness. The meditation practice that helps us to do this is called Vipassana. The Tibetan word for vipassana, *lhag thong*, means "penetrating vision." When awareness penetrates into the unconscious mind to watch the series of mental events that create the phenomena that we unquestionably assume to be the "I," we have taken a big step toward liberating ourselves from its hold on us.

In the beginning, we need to practice Vipassana by applying total concentration on the pageant of events taking place in the theater of the body-mind. With detachment and one-pointedness, we can eventually learn how to catch thoughts just as they begin to emerge, observe their transformations and associations, and notice them passing away in the wake of the next thought. With this acuity, the insidious train of mental events leading to the identification process can be traced and disrupted.

Begin by taking refuge and going into a deep state of tranquil meditation. Next shift your attention from the breath to sensations in the body and thoughts that float through the mind. If you realize that your awareness has been carried away on one of these sensations or thoughts, gently bring it back to its relaxed observation.

When the body is the focus of insight meditation, it is helpful to move your awareness through it in an ordered sequence. You can begin, for example, by placing your awareness on the surface areas of your head, then move to the neck, shoulders, arms, upper back, lower back, buttocks, back and outer thighs, calves and feet. Coming back up the body, begin with the shins, then inner and front thighs, sexual organs, lower abdomen, upper abdomen, chest, neck, etc.

After several days or longer, you can begin moving your awareness through the body in dissecting planes—front to back, top to bottom—being aware of all internal areas and organs. Simply pay attention to various sensations like heat and cold, tension, pain, itching, etc. Focusing your awareness in the body like this may cause feelings and memories associated with particular parts to surface into consciousness. Remain calm, continue to breathe, and observe these phenomena as their trapped energy is released. Just keep letting go.

In a traditional setting, this kind of meditation is practiced intermittently with short walks and rests from early in the morning till late at night for periods of ten days, ninety days, or even longer. Setting aside a whole weekend for a retreat could be an easy way to begin if longer periods are not convenient.

You may also want to use the aura and chakras as objects of insight meditation. Begin by imagining the general outline of the aura around you. Is it mostly in front, more to one side, contracted behind you? What is your overall feeling when you first observe it? Next move your awareness methodically through the aura from the top to the bottom. Pay attention to colors, images, sensations. Do you feel anyone else's energy in your aura? What is he or she doing there?

Placing your awareness in each of the seven chakras now, notice if it feels tight or relaxed. What other sensations or impressions do you experience?

Another approach is to witness the thoughts that arise in your mind. While observing this inner pageant of mental creation, pay attention to whether they are primarily visual or auditory. Do you see only pictures in your mind, or do you talk to yourself? Do you have both pictures and voices? If so, do you have pictures first and then talk to yourself about them, or do you talk to yourself first and then have pictures? Once this is obvious to you, you can imagine that your awareness is the space in which the pictures or sounds are occurring. Finally, you will want to gain insight into the illusory nature of the self identity—who is meditating?[5]

How does the sense of "I" arise? How does it come into play in relationship to internal and external stimulus? The sense of "I" has to be identical with these sensory mechanisms or separate from them. As you observe your various sensory functions, try to decide if one of them (or all of them combined) is the "I." Or if you decide that it is separate from them, then where is it?

---

[5]For more information about insight meditation, see Amadeo Sole-Leris, *Tranquility and Insight* (Boston: Shambhala, 1986).

CHAPTER
FIVE

◆

THE REALM
OF THE
SACRED
SOUND

*A*nahata, the Sankrit name given to the fourth chakra, literally means "not struck." It refers to the subtle vibration that
is the creative energy of the Void. It is chanted as the sacred
syllable OM, and is said to be heard inwardly in meditation when
Kundalini has risen to the heart chakra. The fourth chakra is also
commonly referred to as the heart chakra, defining its position in
the body and hinting at its association with the source of spiritual
inspiration and altruistic love.

The fourth chakra has twelve bright red petals. Inside of this
we find two smoke-colored interlocking triangles. Together they
make the Vayu mandala, which represents the harmonious relationship between the male and female forces of the cosmos.
Inside the Vayu mandala, which also symbolizes the air element,
there is an antelope. Noted for its fleetness, the antelope is a
good vehicle for the ancient god of the wind, Vayu. (See fig. 14
on page 102.)

   In Buddhist Tantra, the fire element is associated with the heart center. Its symbol is a red triangle pointing upwards. Lama Govinda claims that this fire is not physical but psychic. It is the fire of religious devotion and inspiration. He goes on to say that the heart center is the seat of the intuitive mind and transmuted feelings (divine love and compassion), and that it is a primary focus in meditation because it is where the universal is realized in human experience.[1]

   The Primordial Buddha Aksobhya sits on the throne of the heart chakra. (See fig. 15 on page 104.) His Mirror-like Wisdom dispels the illusion of the separateness of things and reflects their innate Voidness. His obscuring passions are anger and aversion.

Figure 14. The fourth chakra, Anahata. The heart chakra has twelve bright red petals. Within the air mandala, two interlacing triangles, we find the seed mantra YAM, which invokes the god of the wind, Vayu. Vayu's vehicle is an antelope.

---

[1]Lama Govinda, *Foundations of Tibetan Mysticism* (York Beach, ME: Samuel Weiser, 1974; and London: Rider & Co., 1974), p. 179.

The alchemical fire of religious devotion and compassion will eventually transform our sense of personal identity. Like the phoenix, the ego will be consumed and transformed. This may be traumatic, often resulting in a severe identity crisis. Nonetheless, the opening of the heart chakra eventually generates a more inclusive form of identity, one where individuality and universality begin to merge.

As the heart chakra awakens, its increased vibrational rate alters the astral body, infusing it with the more sublime energy of the inner heavens. Opening the heart also initiates an intimate relationship with the mystery of life. Each step brings us into a deeper union with the unknown, the infinite potential hidden within each moment, and the beauty, perfection, and distant memory of sublime realms.

In *Journeys Out of the Body*, Robert Monroe describes ecstatic experiences on the astral plane that demonstrate some of these phenomena related to the heart chakra. After he was able to move through the realms of raw emotion on the astral plane, he visited more beautiful regions. He reports being overwhelmed by a "Perfect Environment" in which he experienced a state of pure peace and exquisite emotion. Upon returning to his normal rational self, he felt a profound nostalgia for that place where he knew he belonged and should have always been.[2]

Perhaps you recognize this sublime emotional state. You may have experienced it when standing alone on a mountaintop surrounded by the majesty of the sky and distant landscape. Or it could have been in a deep, silent forest—you stood there in a cathedral of towering trees as shafts of light rainbowed down, God-like, through the richness of the shadows. Or maybe it happened while making love—everything seemed so perfect, so beautiful, so otherworldly.

----

[2]Robert A. Monroe, *Journeys Out of the Body* (New York: Doubleday, 1971), pp. 77–78.

Figure 15. Aksobhya is the lord of the heart chakra and embodies the Mirror-Like Wisdom. His color is white and he rules the Water Element. Like the Shakyamuni Buddha, he displays the Earth-Touching Mudra, the witness mudra. Plate 4 from *Foundations of Tibetan Mysticism*, by Lama Govinda (published in 1974 by Samuel Weiser, York Beach, ME, and Rider & Co., London), reproduced by permission of the publishers.

When the heart center opens fully, an ardent desire for all beings to enjoy the love and beatitude available at this level of awareness is felt. In the Buddhist tradition, this urge is expressed as the vow to assist all sentient beings to reach Enlightenment. A person who actualizes this vow becomes a Bodhisattva.

All forms of romantic love are motivated by this search for union with the source of love. It is a great misfortune that this search is directed outward, and that the source is misunderstood as being a person outside of oneself. The traumatic aftermath of these frustrated projections is an acute sensitivity to the burning longing we experience from being divorced from the true Self and its realm of universal love.

As the heart chakra begins to unfold, it often brings a teacher who serves as the embodiment of this level of consciousness. It may also open us to conscious communication with the spiritual hierarchy of beings guiding the souls of this planet. We may, in turn, act in the heart of a group working to guide terrestrial evolution.

Currently, the energies of the heart chakra are becoming more active as we collectively evolve beyond the stages of consciousness related to the lower three chakras. One problem in this transition, so prevalent in the New Age movement, is the attempt to live in the heart without dealing with the repressions and ego drives in the lower chakras. If, for example, we are angry, arrogant, desperate, or emotionally insecure, love does not flow freely. A forced decision to be loving cannot be the same as a spontaneous outpouring of deeply felt love.

Confusion also arises between romantic love and altruistic love. Romantic love is associated with the projection of the anima and animus and the desire for the perfect relationship. The romance is an ideal. Because it desires to make the other person satisfy a nagging compulsion to feel complete or secure, romantic love is no stranger to manipulative ploys.

Altruistic love, on the other hand, is an empathy and compassion that enables us to act in a deeply caring way. It is an
unconditional acceptance of life and others. There is a depth of
understanding and wisdom in this love that only comes from a
profound suffering and an intense experience of life. It is not
projection or a form of control, but a very sincere openness and
surrender to what is. We may experience disappointments, but
we will never be brokenhearted if we remain open to our potential
for being in this state of love.

As psychic energy flows through the heart center, it has the
capacity to transform and neutralize negative energy. Not only
can we neutralize our own, we can learn how to harmonize
another person's energy. This ability to transform energy in the
heart chakra is used in spiritual and psychic healing. Care should
be taken, however, not to use this healing balm to cover up, or
avoid dealing with, the darker regions of our selves.

We might think that opening the heart center brings only
peace and love. Aside from meeting with our own repressed grief
and fear of being vulnerable, there are many difficulties that arise
as the heart opens. The heart center invokes intense forces from
the soul and inner spiritual realms. The activities, or mere presence, of a person with an enlivened heart center may stimulate
intense defensive reactions in others, as the love vibration penetrates barriers and stirs into resonance the love that has been
buried beneath untold pain and suffering. In *Esoteric Healing*,
Alice Bailey points out that the quandaries accompanying the
opening of the heart chakra are some of the most typical and
problematic experienced on the spiritual path. These include
reactions from others that range from wild devotion to extreme
hatred, causing much confusion and turmoil for the aspirant.[3]

---

[3]Alice Bailey, *Esoteric Healing* (New York: Lucis Publishing Co., 1977), pp.
123–124.

As time goes on we learn not to identify with these reactions and withdraw personal attachments and expectations from this universal love. With compassion and patience, we allow others to accept or reject the forces of love in the heart chakra.

The Alchemical Marriage

The conquest of a dragon or monster by a hero in order to free a maiden is a common theme in mythology. A few familiar heroes are: St. George, who slays a dragon; Theseus, who kills a minotaur to rescue Ariadne from the Cretan labyrinth; and Perseus, who cuts off the head of the gorgon Medusa and overcomes a dragon to free Andromeda. The subsequent romance between the hero and the damsel in distress symbolizes the integration of the fruitful, intuitive, and even mystical aspects of the unconscious related to the heart chakra.

In *The Origin and History of Consciousness*, Neumann shows how, in mythology, the rescued female is no longer associated with the all-powerful and devouring image of the Great Mother. Liberated from her dominance, the maiden is a vulnerable woman with whom the hero (exemplar of the ego) can unite.[4] The hero often has to rebel against conventional (patriarchal) values in order to perform his heroic deeds. These myths obviously depict a male perspective. From a woman's viewpoint, the

---

[4]Erich Neumann, *The Origins and History of Consciousness*, Bollingen Series, Vol. XLII (Princeton, NJ: Princeton University Press, 1970), pp. 195–200.

Figure 16. Coniunctio Sive. Diagram of the mystic marriage of Luna and Sol adapted from the alchemical text *Rosarium Philosophorus*.

successful integration of her male side (animus) empowers her with the heroic strengths needed for her descent into the unconscious. With this strength, she confronts the oppressive aspects of the Great Mother or the Great Father (depending on various mythic renditions) in order to free her essential femininity. Either way, the resulting marriage of the hero and maiden represents an important psychological stage, an individuation from collective forces and the integration of the anima and animus so both individuals can grow.

Archetypal images of this union act as the dynamics behind romantic love. Unfortunately, we rarely understand the import of these as we pursue our quests for the knight in shining armor, or the fairy princess. To gain more insight into this, let's turn briefly to the alchemical tradition that flourished in medieval Europe.

This obscure system, presenting a striking similarity to Tantra, dramatized the transformation of the psyche through a series of rituals, allegories, and contemplations. A major stage in this transformation was symbolized by the Alchemical Marriage. The term used for this mystic marriage, "coniunctio," was used to signify both the mystery of chemical combinations and the marriage of the mystic with God. Alchemy was basically a form of active imagination, the art of communicating with unconscious contents through their projection onto objective reality. Texts and diagrams, used by the alchemists to pursue their metaphorical transformation of various metals and substances, show a king and queen (Sol and Luna) in various activities leading to their coniunctio. We find a good description of these in the alchemical text, *Rosarium Philosophorus*.

In one of the diagrams we find the King and Queen in a sexual embrace as the spirit of the deep rises to engulf them. See fig. 16 on page 108. In this hour of conjunction, the greatest marvel appears; in the bliss of their connubial union, they merge into one another and dissolve. They are made one, as if of one body. The result of this union is a son who is more refulgent and splendid then his parents—he outshines the sun and moon.[5]

The text goes on to remind us that Sol and Luna are two vapors rising from the prima materia as the fire within the alembic increases. Hence, we are not confronted with mere sexual intercourse here, but a higher union.

As we learned in the second chakra, the urge for this mystical union vitalizes romantic encounters and gives quite a punch to the projection of the anima and animus. This often leads to pain and confusion because this synthesis does not take place between two people. Each person has the opportunity, most often misunderstood and therefore lost, of recognizing his or her innate wholeness, and the state of love inherent in it, that has been projected onto the beloved. Though human relationships serve as vehicles for this subjective experience, the Alchemical Marriage is an intrapsychic event.

In Tibetan Tantra, the term Bodhicitta is used to describe the effects of this inner union. Let's see how the Tibetans work toward its unfoldment.

◇

Generation of the Great Compassion

In Sanskrit, *Bodhi* means enlightened, or awakened, consciousness; *citta* has a double connotation, referring to both the mind and the heart. Bodhicitta, therefore, means the Enlightened

---

[5]For more information, see Carl Jung, *Psychology of the Transference* (Princeton, NJ: Princeton University Press, 1966), pp. 85–86.

Mind-Heart manifested when the Great Compassion is experienced. At the heart of Buddhist Tantra are practices and teachings grounded in the intention to manifest Bodhicitta.

This Great Compassion exists, in seed form, in all of us. The Tibetan teachings stress the importance of commitment in the beginning of germinating this tiny grain of compassion. Vows to renounce all forms of activity, physical and psychic, that cause deliberate harm to others and ourselves are one of the ways we express this commitment. All thoughts of failure and negativity, for instance, are seen as immoral because they imply a denial of our own Buddha-nature.

As our little seed of compassion sprouts, great patience is needed to suffer our many imperfections without losing courage and intention. It will take time for the seed of compassion to bear the divine fruit of Bodhicitta. In the meantime, doubt, discouragement, lethargy, and similar feelings are best viewed as opportunities to exercise compassion and commitment. A steady and inexhaustible zeal and faith in the power of compassion is the greatest ally in this endeavor.

Tibetan Tantra then suggests that we meditate on our own suffering. We are encouraged to honestly look at our lives and feel the pain of illnesses, romantic tragedies, emotional traumas, fears, the sense of meaninglessness, material losses, and so on. Everything is in transition, moving through endless cycles of birth and decay. We experience pain as a result of our attempts to maintain a lasting or stable situation in the wake of the fluid nature of the world. In clinging to the notion of ego-consciousness and compulsively striving to satisfy its desires, we stumble through numerous lifetimes, ignorant of our spiritual heritage, fearing and defending ourselves against the heart-wrenching pain of change and loss.

Once we see through the defenses and pride of our egos to the immanence and depth of our own sorrows, we can truly open our hearts to the suffering of our parents, friends, acquaintances, and enemies – and the burden of suffering throughout the world.

Seen from one direction, we feel pain as our concepts, emotional bonds, possessions, and identities are torn away. If we let go and turn around, however, the flux of life is always presenting new and mysterious horizons. The beauty and renewal of creation continually emerge.

See if you can recall your childhood for a moment. Perhaps, like me, you viewed the world with considerable confusion. I couldn't understand why everyone was so unhappy. I remember ardently vowing that I would be happy when I grew up. Within each of us is the ability to know and experience happiness. It is in this part of ourselves that the Great Bliss of Bodhicitta lies buried beneath untold emotional sufferings and mental derangements. To further encourage its growth, Tibetan lamas suggest meditating as if we have attained the perfect status of a Buddha.

One important aspect of becoming one who is awakened (a Buddha) is impartiality – that is, seeing friends and family in the same light as enemies and strangers. All are beings who suffer and yearn for peace and happiness. Through visualization, we can begin to develop impartiality by seeing all beings finding their way to inner peace.

While meditating upon the liberation of all beings from the toils of the world, we can dedicate our lives to removing the weight of their ignorance and suffering. This is not a shallow or idealistic effort, but a deeply heart-felt desire acquired from the insight attained in meditation. It is a courageous task, requiring great integrity. This active part of compassion is the most important, yet it depends on the preceding steps.

Through nourishing others with divine love and truth, we are automatically transported beyond the limitations of personal, self-oriented reality. Beings such as Christ or Buddha are windows into the spiritual depths of us all. The service of such beings demonstrates spiritual forces to those still bound in the ego-world of illusion and suffering. The radiance that shines through them awakens us from our worldly dreams, just as every act of sincere compassion in our own lives dawns upon the world around us.

There was once a monk who was so ugly and deformed that when he went from door to door to beg for alms people would turn him away. He would sometimes feel rejected and have bitter thoughts and retreat to the forest. Buddha, with his omniscience, observed the plight of this monk and manifested himself in a body that was more grotesque than the monk. When the monk saw this wretched creature coming through the forest he was overcome with compassion. This compassion was so profound that the monk experienced enlightenment.

Another important aspect of generating the Great Compassion is becoming more mindful of all forms of desire and negative emotional and mental patterns. In the last chapter, we began observing the normal state of chaos within the mind. Imagine how much psychic energy we need to feed all these mental and emotional mechanisms. Then imagine the additional vital energy used to activate the physical body to respond to all these inner stimuli and you get some idea of how much energy we literally throw away. At the same time, these wayward forces continually push us into the labyrinth of karma.

Once these psychic energies are freed from complexes, defenses, and addictive compulsions, Tantric practices can direct them up the spine to the crown chakra. This reversal of the psychic energy opens the thousand-petaled lotus, flooding the body with a "bliss-creating nectar." In Hindu Tantra, this nectar is mythically associated with the transcendental semen released through the ecstatic union of Kundalini Shakti with her divine lover, Shiva.

Could there be any scientific basis for this bliss-creating nectar? In her book, *Biology*, Helena Curtis reports that scientists speculated in 1972 that the body was capable of manufacturing opiates. In 1975, it was proven that, under certain circumstances, the body produced endogenous opiates (later called endorphines). Four of these endorphines have been chemically analyzed, two of which are found in brain tissue and function to inhibit nerve impulses. The other two are released, like hormones, from the pituitary gland (associated with the crown chakra). One of these pituitary hormones is 48 times stronger than morphine when directly injected into the brain. These opiates have been proven to be generated by meditation, long-distance running, analgesic acupuncture treatments, and the feeling of love.[6]

The Great Bliss (Bodhicitta) is symbolized in Tibetan Tantra by the deity Vajrasattva in meditative sexual embrace with his consort, Vajra Dignity. *Vajra* is Sanskrit for the indestructible and pristine diamond-like quality of Being-Consciousness. Spirit is probably the closest Western concept. In order to perceive this pristine condition, our minds must be open, hence clear of all mental fabrications. The potential for this state of clarity is termed *sattva*, translated literally as essence.

Vajrasattva and his consort are the personification of the purity of consciousness that brings the blissful awareness of Being in its essential pristine and indestructible nature. Their union generates *jnana ambrosia*, or wisdom visualized as a milk-white non-substance, which pours from their hearts and genitals to fill us with Great Bliss as we invoke them in meditation. The analogy of their sexual union expresses the sense of merging we experience when we transcend object/subject parameters to melt into the Great Bliss. Once attained, this level of consciousness fills all forms of relatedness with divine love and compassion.

---

[6]Helena Curtis, *Biology* (New York: Worth Publishers, 1968), p. 162.

◇

Yoga of
Purification and
Bliss

The greatest obstacles we face in acquiring the fullest realization of compassion are self-destructive physical actions and the aura of our negative emotional and mental forces. In the Tibetan Tantric tradition there is a meditation practice especially designed to purge these obscurations. It is called the Yoga of Vajrasattva, and it involves the following four powers, elaborated by John Blofeld in *The Tantric Mysticism of Tibet*:

1. The Power of the "Support"–this is a protective power, which results from aspiring to enter the path leading to the development of Bodhicitta (compassion). By acknowledging the level of awareness that is personified in the form of the Bodhisattva Vajrasattva and taking refuge in this archetype, we are "blessed" and strengthened by the psychic energy embodied within it.

2. The Power of Vanquishing Evil Karma–this is the power of integrity resulting from a genuine and profound remorse for past misdeeds and negative patterns.

3. The Power of Restraining Evil Behavior–this is the power of intention to refrain from misdeeds and negative patterns in the future through a profound realization of the unfortunate karma they produce and how they obscure, like clouds, the ability to bathe in the sun-like warmth of Bodhicitta.

4. The Power of the Antidote—this is the power of for-
giveness and compassion that results from the practices
of the Vajrasattva meditation.[7]

The Vajrasattva meditation is performed as a preliminary
exercise by Tantric neophytes. Later it is used as a means of
purification and initiation into the Vajrasattva level of consciousness. As a preliminary rite, the Hundred Syllable Mantra of Vajrasattva is repeated many times (amounting eventually to a hundred
thousand repetitions in a two-year period) and Vajrasattva is visualized alone. In the more advanced practices, Vajrasattva is visualized with his consort. There are many variations in the Vajrasattva meditation in the various sects of Tibetan Buddhism; the
meditation that follows is a composite of some of the preliminary
and advanced elements of these various schools.

Before beginning the Vajrasattva meditation, the Tibetan
yogis contemplate their personal misdeeds and unfortunate qualities. Thus, after performing the refuge meditation, we ought to
begin by contemplating the many ways we've acted without the
compassion of a Buddha. After this we can affirm our desire to
practice the self-love and honesty necessary to clear these defilements. Sincerely committing ourselves to the goal of generating
Bodhicitta (compassion), we then meditate as follows:

[7]John Blofeld, *The Tantric Mysticism of Tibet* (New York: Dutton, 1970), pp.
160–161.

◇

Vajrasattva
Meditation

In the infinite expanse of the clear blue sky, a white eight-petaled lotus appears above our head at the top of the aura. Upon the lotus, Vajrasattva sits embraced by the Goddess Vajra Dignity. Their bodies are white and transparent. Being insubstantial like moonlight, they emit immeasurable radiance. Both deities are adorned with precious gems (the nature of the Buddha mind) and their garments are of precious silk. He holds a vajra silver bell in his left hand, and in the right a golden vajra scepter. (Together, the bell and scepter represent the feminine and masculine principles associated with wisdom and compassion.) His arms are crossed behind the back of his consort. The left hand of the Goddess holds a skullcap (impermanence), and in her right there is a vajra knife (discriminative mind).

In the center of their heart chakras, which glow like full moons, the electric blue syllable HUM vibrates. It spreads its incandescent light throughout the whole universe. This light penetrates into the hearts of all enlightened beings, who in return, focus their divine compassion back into Vajrasattva and his consort. See fig. 17 on page 118.

Now pray in your own words to Vajrasattva and Vajra Dignity for purification. Next visualize a stream of molten moonlight flowing down from the seed mantra HUM in their hearts and out of the place of their sexual union. It cascades like a waterfall through the stem of the lotus and into the top of your aura. As the top of your aura begins to fill up with their bliss-creating nectar, imagine that it forces all the negativity and darkness to flow out of your aura through a hole in the bottom of it (associated with the first chakra.) In a manner similar to the way you moved your

Figure 17. Vajrasattva and consort Vajra Dignity. Vajrasattva is sometimes considered to be a reflex of the Dhyani Buddha Aksobya; in some sects he is also worshipped as the active expression of the Adibuddha Vajradhara. In the Yoga of Purifications, Vajrasattva and his consort generate the jnana ambrosia, the bliss-creating nectar, that purges the meditator's mind so that the essence of the Void may be perceived. Contemporary painting by Äge Delbanco reproduced by permission of the artist.

awareness through the aura during the insight meditation, be aware of the way the bliss-creating nectar is replacing the various dense and dark areas in the aura. The more you practice this meditation, the more careful you will want to be about making sure that these areas of unclarity are really being released and replaced with Bodhicitta.

Next visualize the white nectar entering the into the crown chakra at the top of your head. Feel it filling your body in the same way it filled your aura. Once again, the longer you practice the more precise you will become in visualizing it purifying the body. At some point, you will want to spend time cleansing every organ in your body. As you become aware of, and release, the tensions, memories, and attitudes lodged in each organ, see and *feel* each one being saturated with bliss-creating nectar. You may want to spend at least one session focusing on each organ in the context of doing the general meditation.

To complete this part of the meditation, imagine the nectar flowing down your spine and out each chakra. Focus on each chakra in sequence, starting at the crown. While repeating one full repetition of the mantra, feel each chakra relaxing and being cleansed by the stream of nectar.

As the nectar pours throughout your body and aura, all your obscurations and sicknesses drain out of your pores, lower orifices, and the bottom of your aura into a hole in the ground. Many black and rotten substances emerge and fall into the earth where the Lord of Death awaits with gaping mouth. Having satisfied his appetite, you are relieved of your noxious substances. (See figure 18 on page 120.)

Now you are shining like a clear crystal filled with the inexhaustible bliss of the milk white nectar of Bodhicitta. From the power of your devotion, Vajrasattva melts into you and his consort is seated on your lap. (As a woman you may reverse these roles. You may also visualize your consort as an incarnation of

Figure 18. Yama and Yami, the Lord of the Dead and his sister, a Buddhist version of the Hindu god of death. Whereas the Hindu god rides a buffalo, the Tibetan version has a buffalo head. Illustration is a closeup from an Avalokiteshvara thanka, 19th century, of the Menri School of central Tibet. From the thanka collection of Sergei Diakoff and reproduced here by permission.

your anima or animus. I have found that this enhances the emotional intensity of this practice considerably.)

OM VAJRASATTVA HUNG–begin reciting this mantra now.

Your body is like a rainbow, manifest yet empty. Like a reflection in a mirror, you are apparent but essentially void of substance. From your heart chakra a tremendous light shines forth. In the center of the radiance in your heart vibrates the electric blue syllable of HUM. From it, brilliant rays of light radiate throughout immeasurable realms purifying all beings.

Spend considerable time seeing your parents, friends, and enemies bathed in the bliss-creating nectar flowing from your heart. See each of these people being filled with, and transformed by, Bodhicitta. Finally you can visualize the entire planet being cleansed and transformed.

You now have a viable alternative to the negative emotional reactions and thought patterns that normally run through your body-mind. With the mindfulness acquired in insight meditation, and the compassion you are cultivating in the Vajrasattva practice, you can begin transforming these negative forces.

Before completing the Vajrasattva meditation, look ahead to several events that you imagine will happen throughout the day. Choose some object or experience to remind you of your commitment to be a Bodhisattva. Visualize yourself in these various settings, acting as if you are Vajrasattva or Vajra Dignity.

When concluding the session, imagine your body dissolving into the HUM. The HUM shrinks until it disappears into the Void, where you remain in meditative equipoise, free of all thoughts and concepts, for as long as you enjoy it. Arising from meditation, offer the merits of your meditation for the benefit of all sentient beings.

When you have a dream in which all manner of foul things are being expelled from you, your Yoga of Purification is having a good effect.[8]

---

[8]For more information on the Vajrasattva practice, you can read Khetsun Sangpo Rinbochay's *Tantric Practice in Nying-Mapa* (Ithaca, NY: Snow Lion, 1982), or John Blofeld's *The Tantric Mysticism of Tibet* (NY: Dutton, 1970).

CHAPTER
SIX

◆

THE GREAT
PURIFICATION

*T*he Sanskrit name for the fifth chakra is *Vissudha*, meaning cleansed or purified. Its element is ether–the space-substance out of which the other four elements are crystallized. Inside its lotus of sixteen petals we find the Akasa mandala, an inverted triangle or *yoni*, which represents the feminine powers of creation. Inside the Akasa mandala, there is another white elephant holding one of his seven trunks up in the air, perhaps heralding our triumph over the instinctive forces of the lower chakras. See fig. 19 on page 124.

In Buddhist Tantra, the throat chakra is associated with the air element and symbolized by a green crescent moon. Air is here related to movement and wind, and according to Lama Govinda, it not only represents the vital qualities of the breath, but the origin of all sounds and spiritual vibrations. From these come the specific attributes of all things, and hence, all forms of distinguishing knowledge.[1] Amitabha, the Primordial Buddha whose wisdom energy is Discriminating Wisdom, therefore sits on the throne of

---

[1]Lama Govinda, *Foundations of Tibetan Mysticism* (York Beach, ME: Samuel Weiser, 1974; and London: Rider & Co., 1974), p. 183.

the fifth chakra. His obscuring passion is greed. (See fig. 20 on page 126.)

Located in the throat, the fifth chakra functions as a communication center. Like a telephone switchboard, the throat chakra is the mediator between the incoming and outgoing calls of the nervous system. When the communication is more than the neurological circuits can handle, or when there is conflict between mental and emotional stimuli, the circuits overload and the body responds with tension in the neck and shoulders.

When a constellation of pain and confusion has formed around the emotional or physical body over considerable time, and the mental body and brain have learned to shut off or repress stimuli that activate the memory patterns associated with the original traumas, the mind may become completely divorced

Figure 19. The fifth chakra is Visuddha. Inside the lotus of sixteen smoky purple petals we find the Akasa mandala, a white circle representing the Ether Element. It is inside the Trikona, a downward pointing triangle symbolic of the feminine power of creation. The seed mantra for the ether element is HAM.

from physical reality (psychosis). Less severe constrictions result from unexpressed feelings or communications. Clairvoyant analysis of the fifth chakra often reveals the need to express repressed emotions. Difficulty in organizing thoughts and expressing them, verbally or in writing, also indicates constriction in the fifth chakra.

Prayer, in its true sense, is a form of communication between the personality and other dimensions of the psyche. Prayers are thought forms that can be filled with information from deeper levels of the psyche and from spiritual beings on the inner planes. Out of a realization of the impoverished condition of the ego, we pray for guidance. Most people misunderstand prayer to be asking—or in many instances, demanding—"God" to fulfill our desires.

Prayer is best thought of as a way of asking for what is best from the highest part of our nature. It is a way of becoming vulnerable to inspirational forces, of creating a vessel for receiving the rain of grace falling from the spiritual dimensions within. Jungian analyst John Sanford, in *Healing and Wholeness*, points out that prayer is an instinct, and psychologically speaking, a way of orienting the ego-self to the Self. He goes on to say that the positive results of prayer are not related to our personal beliefs about God; what is important is that we address ourselves to the "Higher Power," whatever our concept of it might be.[2]

Perhaps we could say that the contemporary correlation to the misuse of prayer is the use of affirmations. There are a number of different teachings today that encourage a willful repetition of positive or idealized statements. One unfortunate effect that I have witnessed in this use of affirmations is a polarization between conscious ideals and unconscious belief systems and emotional programming. If we fail to divulge, lovingly accept, and

---

[2]John A. Sanford, *Healing and Wholeness* (New York: Paulist Press, 1977), p. 133.

Figure 20. Amitabha is the lord of the fifth chakra and embodies Discriminative Wisdom. His color is red and his element is Fire. His hands rest in his lap in the Dhyana (meditation) Mudra. Plate 3 from *Foundations of Tibetan Mysticism* by Lama Govinda (published in 1974 by Samuel Weiser, York Beach, Maine, and Rider & Co., London) reproduced here by permission of the publishers.

effectively change unconscious imprints, these forceful tactics of the ego-self create tension and resistance in the unconscious that may lead to a dangerous split between the conscious and unconscious minds.

One of the themes of the fifth chakra is communication. In the relationship between the unconscious and conscious self, we need to begin thinking in terms of a permeable membrane that allows a mutual exchange. From the conscious side, we need to listen to the personal unconscious so we can understand "where it's coming from." With this understanding we can sort out the programming that is inappropriate. Erasing these old programs, and replacing them with growth enhancing parameters, in turn gives us access to the guidance of the collective unconscious. Eventually this membrane will dissolve as the ego identity merges with the transpersonal Being of the Self.

We are continually creating our private world with desires, thoughts, and prejudices. The more we evolve in consciousness, the more our individual reality is aligned and unified with the whole of existence. It is not that we become better at creating our reality, but that we change our viewpoint. Changing sides, ego-to-Cosmos, is the greatest affirmation.

The fifth chakra is also associated with clairaudience or mental telepathy, psychic communication with other people or with disincarnate beings. Other clairaudient experiences include hearing and understanding inner sounds. For instance, some people experience psychic energy as clairaudient tones when doing psychic readings or healing work. Composers and musicians also have heightened clairaudient ability. They often write or improvise music that they hear with the inner ear.

The principle of inner music – the knowledge that sound carries meaning and structures psychic energy – underlies the use of mantras or sacred chants. Certain musical, vocal, and inner sounds have the ability to change and affect the patterns of energy in the etheric and other subtle bodies. When used properly, these sounds can manifest situations and alter physical forms. Music can be used in healing, and mantras and chants can open psychic channels and create specific psychological and spiritual states of consciousness.

The power of the voice is available to us in everyday life, although we rarely appreciate or develop it. For example, after years of working with clients, Milton Erickson, a well-known hypnotherapist, was able to give a hypnotic suggestion without inducing a trance. In a few skillfully delivered words, he could reverse deep-seated neurotic patterns and utterly transform a person's life. A being with great spiritual power, or one especially trained in the art of using the human voice, can produce miraculous effects. The fifth chakra and the voice can also express the intention or creative purpose of the deeper layers of the psyche and, through mediumship, of spiritual entities.

The voice contains a great deal of information about a person. Emotional qualities are readily discernable in the sound and inflection of the voice. Attitudes, psychological postures, and mental orientation are also clearly evident in speech patterns and vocabulary. Oriental medicine recognizes this relationship and considers voice analysis to be an important part of diagnosis.

One way we can become more effective in life is by communicating more clearly. So often we give double messages. While asking for something verbally, we are thinking or feeling "I don't deserve this," or "they won't give it to me anyway." Say what you mean and ask clearly for what you want. Perhaps the secret to real communication lies in the ability to listen—to ourselves as well as to others.

The fifth chakra is also related to the more mundane functions of the mental body. This lower mind is the practical and logical aspect of the mental processes. It is this level of the mind that categorizes facts and calculates figures. In generating concepts and structures, it gives symbolic representation to subjective states of awareness, creating a language through which they can be objectified and communicated.

Pragmatic intuition (intuition concerned with practical things) is another faculty associated with the fifth chakra. For instance, when the telephone rings, our pragmatic intuition may tell us who is calling. It may also inform us about such mundane considerations as whether to take a chance and go to the beach on a day when it seems to be too cold or windy, or which car we should buy.

The fifth chakra marks the passage of consciousness into the realm of reflective awareness. Beyond the instinctive, reactional, and habitual modes of mental activity, the reflective level offers the ego-self new dimensions of abstract thought and greater powers to control or direct willfully the events and processes of life.

The Mantra of Compassion

The use of mantras in Eastern religious disciplines is a very potent and articulate application of the power of sound and the principle behind affirmations. Mantras are sound-symbols which activate spiritual forces within the psyche. Various seed syllables and combinations of syllables evoke specific psychic states through their vibrational patterns and meter. One of the most widely known mantras is OM MANI PADME HUM. Many Tibetan lamas consider it to be the greatest of mantras. It is the mantra of the Bodhisattva Avalokiteshvara and galvanizes the wisdom and power of compassion. The mantra and the visualiza-

Figure 21. Avalokiteshvara. In this form, he has four arms and one face, and embodies the Great Compassion (Karuna) of the Enlightened Mind. OM MANI PADME HUM is his mantra. From the Thanka collection of Sergei Diakoff, reproduced here by permission.

tion of the Bodhisattva of compassion are a means to call upon and focus this force of the transpersonal level of the psyche.

Writing on the mantra of Avalokiteshvara, Lama Govinda, in *The Foundation of Tibetan Mysticism*, explains that *OM* symbolizes the origin and sum of all sounds in the universe. As the tonic note of the cosmos, it represents the harmony of the spheres and is considered to be the supreme or sacred sound. *MANI PADME* means the jewel in the lotus, or the Void within manifestation. It expresses the balance of all pairs of opposites and the essential divinity within each of us. *HUM* is a word of power that removes the veils of ego-bound awareness. Whereas OM represents the ascent toward universality, HUM is the descent of the universal into consciousness.[3]

Govinda goes on to say that the meaning of a mantra like OM MANI PADME HUM cannot be exhausted by analyzing its component parts, especially in this brief description. It is said that this great mantra contains the living synthesis of the five wisdoms (associated with the five Dhyani Buddhas). It therefore embraces and concentrates the fundamental truths of Tibetan Tantra.[4]

According to legend, Avalokiteshvara, the Bodhisattva of Compassion, was looking down from the peaceful celestial realms upon the suffering and confusion in the worlds of illusion. He was filled with such intense compassion that his thoughts, generating the desire for the liberation of all beings, caused his head to burst into innumerable heads. From his body sprang a thousand helping hands. In each palm an eye appeared. Thus the compassion of a Bodhisattva is not blind emotion, but love combined with wisdom; the wisdom of the inner oneness of all life leading to the capacity to feel the suffering of the world and of others as if it were our own. (See figure 21.)

---

[3]Govinda, *Foundations of Tibetan Mysticism*, p. 213.
[4]Govinda, *Foundations of Tibetan Mysticism*, p. 223.

John Blofeld, in *Mantras, Sacred Words of Power*, tells a beautiful Chinese story that is typical of tales told to demonstrate the power of Avalokiteshvara's mantra. A cruel warlord fleeing from battle takes refuge in a small hermitage where only a young serving-boy and an old lama lived. After he forced them to fill his saddlebags with valuables from the temple, he ordered them to make him a bed in the shrine hall. There he fell asleep near the statue of Kuan Yin (a Chinese rendition of Avolokiteshvara). The old lama, feeling great compassion for this wayward visitor and his folly, sat nearby and chanted the mantra *OM MANI PADME HUM* in a low hum all through the night.

The warlord had many dreams in which he enjoyed much happiness in previous lives with others who were very kind and loving to him. Each of these pleasant dreams was followed by one in which the people who had cared for him were now his victims in his present life. In these dreams he suffered the heart-wrenching pain of shooting, beheading, or in some other way torturing and abusing those peoples who had been so kind to him.

He awoke drenched in sweat and full of remorse. He fell before the statue of Kuan Yin and beat his head on the flagstone floor. When the lama served him breakfast, the warlord bowed to him and begged to be accepted as his student.

The lama refused him saying that the monastic life was not for him. He told him to ride on his way encouraging him to use his power and whatever wealth he might acquire for the welfare of the oppressed, for everyone had been his mother or father or good friend in a previous life.

Startled by the similarity of the lama's words and his night of dreams, the warlord beseeched the lama to give him something to hold on to in his life ahead. The lama told him there is nothing stronger than the power of compassion. If his courage faltered because of the burden of his evil karma, he should let the power of the mantra *OM MANI PADME HUM* give him the strength not to give in to his cruelty.

After shamefully returning the belongings of the temple, he departed. It is said that some of his exsubordinates once recognized him working as a muleteer for a community of monks in the remote hermitage on Wu T'ia's southern peak.[5]

$$\Diamond$$

Dream Yoga

Dreams have puzzled the conscious mind throughout history—the modern scientific community is no exception. Various schools of psychotherapy have their own explanations and techniques for analyzing and deciphering dreams. In ancient cultures, they were thought to take the dreamer to supernatural worlds where gods and demons lived. It was considered very foolish to disregard the mandates of the gods met in the dreamworld. In some cultures there were sacred places and rituals that people could use to call upon these gods in times of need. For example, there were approximately four hundred dream temples in ancient Greece. People could sleep in the temple to obtain guidance or healing from the indwelling god or goddess. A similar practice took place in ancient Egypt.

Many dreams are reflections of the inner heavens in the pools of our personal psyches. In our everyday consciousness, we

---

[5]John Blofeld, *Mantras, Sacred Words of Power* (London: Unwin Hyman, 1977), pp. 34–35.

organize events and perceptions within the framework of our familiar three-dimensional space and time. Our rational experience is further limited by cultural and personal conceptual patterns. The greater psyche knows no such limitations. This is why it's so difficult to understand the events and symbols that shine down from these realms. Nonetheless, we may someday agree with Aborigine tribes who believe that dream time is more important than waking life. They believe that life, as we know it, is an event being dreamed by Something Else.

Dreams are a great source of insight and healing; they transfer information back and forth between the various levels of our inner selves. Experiences from the outer world are digested in dreams, while events and processes taking place on all dimensions of the psyche are metabolized. Our dreams have a much greater impact on our waking lives than we realize.

The greater psyche spans the past and future. Dreams therefore are composed of an incredible integration of information and experience – spiritual guidance, precognition, out-of-body experiences, telepathy with incarnate and disincarnate beings, archetypal dramas, inspiration, self-reflection, humor, wild fantasies, past-life and childhood memories, desires, fears, compensations, bodily processes, "noise" in the nervous system, and as Jung said, "heaven knows what besides." These are all dramatized in symbols and metaphors – some of which may never be understood by the rational mind – that galvanize certain psychological factors and create or draw us into the various kinds of physical events that we meet in our waking life.

Trance medium Jane Roberts, in *The Nature of the Psyche*, channeled Seth's insights about how we can witness the creation of external events by the psyche in the dream state. He uses the metaphor of the ocean forming waves to show how the inner workings of the psyche splash out into the realm of our waking awareness. He goes on to propose that through the creation of events, the psyche experiences its own reality in the same way that we hear our own voice by talking.[6]

Seth explains how the ego-self also has a hand in the shaping of its own fate. Its emotional patterns, preconceptions, and habits, to various degrees, resonate with only a small number of the predilections of the greater psyche. It is through these that some events manifest while others remain mere probabilities.[7]

To begin exploring the dream state, we need to become better at remembering dreams. A small pillow filled with the herb mugwort stimulates dream recall, as will a few drops of a tincture made from the herb kava kava taken before bedtime. Vitamin B complex has also been recommended to improve dream memory. Upon retiring, look forward to the adventures that await you in dreamland and tell yourself to remember your dreams.

When you awaken, at any time during the night or in the morning, lie still with closed eyes and relive as many dream events as you can remember. Don't be concerned about their sequence. As you go over the images again and again, you will find yourself recalling more and more details and scenes. At this stage, concentrate only on the feelings in the images. Record these feelings and images accurately on a tape or in a journal, still without attempting to analyze them. Practice reliving these dreams in the way that a child listens to a story. Allow the meanings of these stories to emerge spontaneously, rather than through rational interpretation.

The problem with most psychoanalytical methods of dealing with dreams is that they involve only the conscious ego. As we have seen, the dream is an experiential realm beyond the world of the ego, its true significance is often lost by reducing it to the

---

[6]Jane Roberts, *The Nature of the Psyche* (Englewood Cliffs, NJ: Prentice Hall, 1979), p. 130.
[7]Roberts, *The Nature of the Psyche*, pp. 136–141.

ego's frame of reference. Direct participation in the dream is, therefore, a superior approach.

You may have had the experience of "waking up" in a dream. To your surprise, you were able to reason, and perhaps even act willfully, once you realized that you were dreaming. These lucid dreams can seem just as real as normal life, or may cause us fear when we cannot recognize the surroundings. Because lucid dreams seem very much like memories of actual events, they were dismissed by scientists until recent research at Stanford University. Stanford dream researcher Dr. Stephen La Berge devised a method whereby lucid dreamers could send messages to the outside world while asleep. When the dreamers became aware of dreaming, they moved their eyes in a prearranged manner (brainwave patterns proved that they were asleep).[8]

In the practice of Dream Yoga, Tantric yogis concentrate the meditating mind on dreams. One of the basic propositions of the Tibetan Buddhists is that incarnation is an auspicious occasion, an opportunity to be appreciated and used diligently, the dream state is no exception. According to these teachings, the most serious consequences of thoughts and actions are the conditions they create in the psyche. The Tibetan teachings attach considerable importance to the unconscious mind. They recognize that the manifestation of these more esoteric aspects of the psyche are restrained by the roles, social conditions, and defenses of everyday life. The value of the dream state is that we are released from these restraints. Attention to conduct as well as the environmental gestalt of the dream state, therefore, offers us an excellent opportunity for self-knowledge.

Dream yoga is essentially an extension of the Buddhist discipline of Insight Meditation. If practiced in everyday life, this mindfulness will be easier to carry over into the nocturnal realms

---

[8]Stephen La Berge, *Lucid Dreaming* (New York: Ballantine, 1985), p. 80.

of consciousness. In the Tibetan tradition, there are a number of techniques used in dream yoga.

During the day it is important to maintain a strong desire to recognize the dream state. It is therefore helpful to dwell in a solitary place and still the mind during the day, so there can be more continuity from day to nighttime consciousness. To further strengthen our intention, we are guided to practice seeing waking experiences as if they were dreams.

Maintaining awareness while falling asleep is another important skill to be mastered. There are several variations of the technique to accomplish this in the Tantric tradition: here is a simple one. Visualize a brilliant red AH in the central channel at your throat chakra while entering into the nocturnal realms. Maintain a keen awareness of it. Ignoring distracting ramblings of the mind, keep in mind the illusionary qualities of phenomenal existence. After consistent practice, you will eventually be able to remain aware as you pass through the region of hypnogogic images to enter into the world of dreams.

In deep sleep the vital airs (prana) collect in the heart and root chakras. When the vital airs move to the throat and sacral chakras, dreams arise. When the vital airs rise to the solar plexus and head chakras we wake up. Concentrating on the throat center therefore causes the prana of the heart center to be weaker so that sleep will be lighter and awareness clearer. Dreams produced through focusing on the throat chakra supposedly last longer, hence we can practice dream yoga for a longer time.

Another factor related to the quality of awareness during sleep is connected to the amount of air flowing through the left or right nostril. Lying on the right side while falling asleep encourages more air to pass through the right nostril which in turn activates the left hemisphere of the brain, stimulating the rational qualities of the left hemisphere and enhancing our ability to be "awake" during dreaming.[9]

It is also helpful to sleep only for short periods of time. Each time you wake up, review whether or not you were aware while you were dreaming. Fall back to sleep while reviewing any dreams you may remember with your attention focused on your visualization in the throat chakra. You can also say to yourself, "I will wake up in my dreams." Repeat this several times with conviction.

In La Berge's research at Stanford it was discovered that most lucid dreams occur during REM periods (rapid eye movement) and that the frequency and duration of REM sleep increases in the later part of the night's sleep. The early morning hours, after a good night's sleep, are therefore the most auspicious for the practice of dream yoga.

At some point in your practice you will wake up in a dream. Suddenly you will realize, "This is a dream! I'm dreaming!" In Carlos Castaneda's *Journey to Ixtlan*, about his experiences with the Sorcerer Don Juan, Carlos was instructed to remember to look at his hands when he became lucid during a dream. Don Juan was showing him a way to "stabilize his dream body."[10] Once you have managed to wake up in a dream, the next task is how to remain aware.

One of the problems that La Berge found in his research was that we often have a tendency to physically wake up once the lucid dream begins, especially when the emotional content is threatening or intense.

Emotional conflict is often the source of the premature ending of a lucid dream. For example, lucid dreams often are related to sexual experiences. If a person is sexually inhibited, he or she

---

[9]For more information about dream yoga, see Charles Muses, *Esoteric Teachings of Tibetan Tantra* (York Beach, ME: Samuel Weiser, 1961), pp. 200–220.
[10]Carlos Castaneda, *Journey to Ixtlan* (New York: Pocket Books, 1975).

will normally nip a lucid dream of sexual content in the bud by waking up rather than allowing the experience consciously. In *Lucid Dreaming*, La Berge explains that in order to overcome this obstacle it is helpful to change our conscious attitudes so that we are less inhibited.[11]

Some people become too emotionally involved, which may cause us to lose our objectivity and become identified with the dream self. In both cases emotional detachment is important. La Berge's solution is simple: "Don't panic! Remain calm."[12]

Once you have learned to remain awake in a dream, Tibetan teachings encourage us to exercise our will to alter the dream experience. After becoming adept in changing dream content, Tibetan yogis transform themselves into meditational deities and travel to their mandala abodes. On the astral plane, the principal building blocks of reality are mental and emotional configurations. By transforming the objects and events of the dream, we realize the essential insubstantiality of these aspects of ourselves.

In *Lucid Dreaming*, La Berge shares one of his own dream experiences to illustrate the therapeutic effects of transforming the dream environment. Dreaming he was in the middle of a classroom riot, a large bully with a pockmarked face had him in an iron grip from which he was trying to escape. When he recognized that he was dreaming, he recalled that he had learned to stop struggling in other similar situations. Then he realized the struggle was a dream and the conflict was within himself. He then had a lucid awareness that the repulsive bully was a dream personification of something he was denying inside himself. He also realized that inner harmony would prevail only through accepting whatever the barbarian represented. His first attempt to feel loving toward his ogre failed, and he was overcome with disgust for the bully. He tried to ignore his visceral reactions and seek love in

---

[11]La Berge, *Lucid Dreaming*, pp. 118–120.
[12]La Berge, *Lucid Dreaming*, p. 118.

his heart. When he did this, he looked the barbarian in the eyes and words of acceptance flowed out. The ogre then melted into him and the riot disappeared. The dream ended here and La Berge awoke feeling wonderfully calm.[13]

Keep in mind that our mind is actually a dream world, too. Our waking experience, like a dream, is not a solid or absolute reality, but is essentially metaphorical. We act out our psychological dramas with co-actors with whom we are karmically connected, or with whom we at least share a karmic resonance. As in the dream state, we don't have to suffer from our interpretations of these events—we are free to change how we perceive and respond to them. Until we become Buddhas (awakened), it is helpful to remember that we are dreaming.

The practice of dream yoga is ultimately used to enter higher states of consciousness. Transforming ourselves into the various deities, in a manner similar to our meditation practices, and concentrating one pointedly in their states of contemplation on the Clear Light of the Void, is the goal of Dream Yoga.

I have received spiritual guidance, encountered Tantric deities, and enjoyed many mystical experiences on the astral plane while asleep. I would like to share one of these experiences now, and mention several others later in the book.

In a lucid dream, I was once taken by a spirit guide on a journey down my spine. I saw how the world looked through each chakra. I experienced each level of consciousness and how it is conditioned by the pictures and programs associated with it. Through the crown chakra, I then ventured into radiant realms and finally merged into a beautiful white-golden light. It was many years later before I returned to this level of awareness in meditation.

---

[13]La Berge, *Lucid Dreaming*, pp. 12–13.

◇

Death,
Transfiguration,
and Rebirth

Closely related to practice of dream yoga, *The Tibetan Book of the Dead* trains a yogi to recognize the Clear Light of the Void at the moment of death, and thus attain liberation. Before we explore the after-death state, and the meditation practices that prepare us to make the best use of it, let's refer once again to Jungian psychology to explore the universal occurrence of the death initiation.

In the evolution of the ego-self, consciousness is consolidated into an individual, but temporal, structure. There is, however, an inherent drive within us to transcend this limitation. Before this can happen the old self must die. The transfiguration of the "I" that happens at this stage is universally related to a death initiation in myth and religion. In myth, the death of the hero leads to a rebirth (resurrection) of a god or immortal being. The death, resurrection, and ascension of Jesus is a perfect example of how this mythogem is often projected onto religious heroes.

In the ancient Egyptian cult of Osiris, we find another good example of initiation through a death experience. Patterned after the myth of Osiris, which describes how Osiris was united with the sun god Ra to become immortal through dying, neophytes were placed in a sarcophagus for a number of days. During this time they experienced many trials on the inner planes. If successful (indeed, some never returned to their bodies), the initiate brought back knowledge from beyond death.

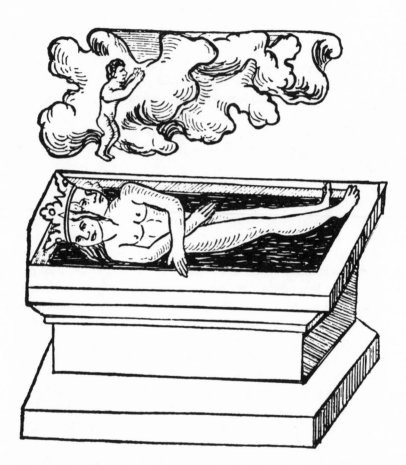

Figure 22. Animae Extractio Vel. A drawing from the alchemical text, *Rosarium Philosophorus*, depicting the death and purification (putrefication per au) of the merged bodies of Luna and Sol while the soul ascends.

In *The Psychology of the Transference*, Jung considered the trans-figuration of the ego-self represented in the alchemical diagram from the Rosarium Philosophorum following the coniunctio that we referred to in the heart chakra.

Death: Here King and Queen are lying dead. In great distress the soul is sped. (Rosarium)[14] Having merged into a single body, the divine couple is placed in a coffin. (See fig. 22 on page 142.) Also referred to as "putrefaction" in alchemical texts, this stage symbolizes the state of dissolution where the aggregates that compose the ego-self are dissipated. On the dark side of this psychological phase, we may suffer a disillusionment with the apparent emptiness of life. If we don't understand this process of decay, we might foolishly seek out old ego patterns. Or, if the urge for transformation has been perverted, we might find ourselves contemplating suicide.

A desire to die may arise when the path to individuation is blocked by attitudes of the ego-self. Suicidal impulses, in this case, are symbolic communications from the unconscious that the attitudes standing in the way of our spiritual transformation must die. In addition to foreknowledge, or even spiritual or psychological assistance, this takes a lot of courage. The "dying" process is terrifying to the ego-self; the birth of the transpersonal identity that follows is unimaginable, or at best doubtful, to the dying self.

Jungian therapist John Sanford, in *Healing and Wholeness*, points out that the death initiation may also occur in the guise of a debilitating illness. He explains how our relationship to the archetypal forces at this level of the psyche is a delicate matter. These

---

[14]Quoted from Carl Jung, *The Psychology of the Transference* (Princeton, NJ: Princeton University Press, 1966), p. 95. There are also a number of publications about alchemy that you can explore since the interest in this material is developing again today.

potent configurations, like the gods and goddesses of ancient religions, are very temperamental. If we ignore or disrespect them we may incur their wrath. Thus, any number of mysterious psychological disorders or physical diseases force the conscious self into a period of withdrawal and incubation. This type of illness can dissolve the crystallized ego structure, allowing new aspects of the psyche to emerge during the convalescence.

Sanford goes on to give examples of how illness may serve as an initiation in lives of primitive healers. Shamans are often called to their vocation through an initiatory illness. During an intense psychological crisis or physical illness, the shaman to be (male or female) experiences being carried away by the demons of illness and death. A return to health occurs only after the person accepts the communication from the spirit world about what kind of life he or she is to pursue.[15]

Jung found also that the mystery of the death initiation may be enacted in a dream. In *Aion* he presented the following example: a young man dreams of climbing a mountain. At the top he sees an altar and a sarcophagus with a statue of himself upon it. A veiled priest, carrying a staff with a living sun-disk on it, then approaches him. All of a sudden he realizes that he is dead. He feels deprivation and fear instead of the sense of achievement he felt from climbing the mountain. As he bathes in the warm rays of the sun-disk however, he feels rejuvenated and strong.

Jung points out that this dream shows the distinction between initiation and the hero myth. The act of climbing is like a trial of strength associated with the will to achieve ego consciousness in the heroic phase. The young patient thought therapy would be an heroic undertaking. The dream scene by the altar corrected this mistaken assumption. By seeing himself dead and entombed, the dream taught that he must submit to a power

---

[15]Sanford, *Healing and Wholeness*, pp. 64–65.

greater than himself. Only through his death initiation and this submission could he experience rebirth.[16]

In Tibetan Tantra, death–in its most literal sense–is employed as an initiation. *The Tibetan Book of the Dead* (Bardo Thodol, or "Book of Liberation Through Hearing on the After-Death Plane") poetically describes how, after we have left the body at death, we sojourn through the inner realms (the Bardo, literally "inbetween state") and encounter various wrathful and peaceful deities. If we can identify with the Clear Light of the Void and maintain the awareness that all that we experience is illusionary, we attain liberation. If we are unable to do this, we are controlled by karmic forces that pull us eventually back into another physical body.

There are three phases, or Bardo states, that we pass through after death on our return to another incarnation. According to Joseph Campbell, in *The Mythic Image*, the first stage, "Intermediate State of the Moment of Death" (Chikhai Bardo), is related to the states of consciousness of the awakened sixth and seventh chakras. After the moment of death, we might not realize that we have separated from the body. In our confusion, or even trance-like sleep, we normally don't recognize the Clear Light of the Void, or remain in its purity without being distracted by thoughts. Thus for the untrained, this first stage of the afterlife gives way to the second phase.

The Choyid Bardo, or The Intermediate State of Glimpsing Reality, relates to the psychological functions of the fifth chakra. Waking up in the second stage and realizing that we have died, we are frightened by the brilliance of the light radiating from the Five Wisdom Energies (the five Dyhani Buddhas) and turn to the dimmer light of the hallucinations of our minds. What we have thought and done while in the body floods our consciousness in

---

[16]Carl Jung, *Aion*, Bollingen Series, Vol. IX (Princeton, NJ: Princeton University Press, 1959), p. 194.

numerous dream-like experiences. The Tibetan teachings repeatedly remind us, however, that what we see at this stage is a projection of our own mental content. The practice of dream yoga is obviously a good preparation for the knowledge and concentration needed at this time.

The last stage, "The Intermediate State of Seeking Rebirth" (Sidpa Bardo), has two sub-stages that correspond to the awareness of the fourth chakra and chakras three, two, and one.[17] The Buddhists maintain that at first we enjoy happy visions and reap the fruit of our impulses and aspirations of our higher nature. As these forces exhaust themselves, we descend through the inner realms where visions born of our lower nature arise. Though these terrify us, we are inseparable from them and cannot escape.

As the experiences become more lustful and sensual, we feel an overpowering desire for the life of the flesh. Thus the attachment to the reality that we know, and our karmic predilections, pull us down into the third stage of the afterlife, the intrauterine life.

The purpose of the Bardo Thodol is to teach us to hold onto the vision of the Clear Light in the first stage. If we can do this, then only the more spiritual experiences of the first stage need be encountered before we pass onto other realms of existence or choose to be reborn as a Buddha without breaking the continuity of consciousness.

If we fail to attain liberation in the first stage, then we begin to descend through the six realms of existence. The pantheon of deities found in these various realms (in the Bardo Thodol) represent the universal forces active on the different levels of the psyche. Their appearance in the mythology of the after-death

---

[17]Joseph Campbell, *The Mythic Image*, Bollingen Series, Vol. C (Princeton, NJ: Princeton University Press, 1974), p. 394.

state symbolizes the stages and forces that occur on the path of psychic development.

If we are unable to hold the Clear Light in the first stage, we can still gain liberation by taking refuge in the five Dhyani Buddhas, which appear one after another in the second Bardo. By giving up the delusions of our minds, its various elements can be transformed into the Wisdom Energy of each of the five Dhyani Buddhas. Realizing that the temporal forms of the body-mind are not who we are, we awaken to the Eternal Clear Light of the Void and experience the Dharmakaya (body of truth).

If we have not been liberated at this time because of the stubborn forces of the unconscious mind that have controlled us for many lifetimes—and that now still cause us to wander downward—then on the sixth day the five Dhyani Buddhas and their consorts and attendants appear simultaneously. (See fig. 23 on page 148.)

If, however, we fail to hold on to the Clear Light and continue to indulge ourselves in the illusions of our mind, on the seventh day the Knowledge Holders (Vidyadharas) appear. These five deities and their consorts manifest along with a host of dakinis and their attendants, all of which make up the mandala of the Knowledge Holders. If we realize that these spiritual teachers have come to lead us to the "Pure Realm of Space," and focus our minds on their five colored lights, Liberation can now be attained.

Failing to accomplish this, the previous deities are transformed into fifty-eight blood-drinking deities. This mandala of the wrathful deities (see fig. 24 on page 149) represents the mental strengths needed to overcome the delusions and passions of the ego-self. The average person will most probably continue to fall into the lower realms, attempting to escape from these terrifying deities. But a Tantric yogi, having visualized these wrathful deities in meditation, recognizes them and merges him/

Figure 23. The Great Mandala of the Peaceful Deities. This mandala depicts the five Dhyani Buddhas appearing with their consorts and is used in conjunction with the meditation practices associated with *The Tibetan Book of the Dead*. Illustration from *The Tibetan Book of the Dead*, by W. Y. Evans-Wentz. Copyright 1960 by W. Y. Evans-Wentz. Reprinted by kind permission of Oxford University Press, New York and London.

Figure 24. The Great Mandala of the Knowledge-Holding and Wrathful Deities. This mandala contains the wrathful manifestations of the five Dhyani Buddhas used in the meditation practices associated with *The Tibetan Book of the Dead*. Illustration from *The Tibetan Book of the Dead*, by W. Y. Evans-Wentz. Copyright 1960 by W. Y. Evans-Wentz. Reprinted by kind permission of Oxford University Press, New York and London.

herself with them. Assimilating their attributes, Liberation is finally gained by the yogi.

The Bardo Thodol is based on the premise that through the portals of death we enter the same realms of consciousness that we access in advanced stages of meditation. If we maintain a high level of clarity and purpose at the time of death, we have an opportunity to join the community of those enlightened souls who have Thus Gone Beyond (Tathagatas).

Jung was fascinated by the *Bardo Thodol*, and wrote in his "Psycholological Commentary" to the Evans-Wentz edition that he was greatly inspired by its deep insights into the nature of the human psyche. He confides that our Western psychology has only explored the lowest of the three levels of the psyche that correspond to the after-death states. Western science, therefore, has the two remaining subtler regions to discover.[18]

$$\Diamond$$

Cutting Attachments

The path of liberation leading up from the fifth chakra is very steep. Like a mountain climber, we need the proper equipment for the ascent. According to Buddhist Tantra, there are three important provisions for this journey: the enlightened motive of compassion (which we studied in the last chapter), the correct view of voidness (which we will study later), and the renounced mind.

---

[18]Carl Jung, "Psychological Commentary," in *The Tibetan Book of the Dead*, W. Y. Evans-Wentz, ed. (New York & London: Oxford University Press, 1960), pp. xxxvi, xiii–xliii.

For most of us, the word renounce has negative associations; perhaps images of monks or nuns living austere lives come to mind. But the Buddhist act of renunciation is not the practice of denying objects or appetites; it is giving up belief in the ego-self.

Our attachment to the ego-self, composed of the deluded ramifications of the five wisdom energies, keeps us trapped in the world of illusion, called Samsara in Tantra. In Sanskrit, *Samsara* literally means to circle. It refers to the round of existence (the wheel of birth and death). Samsara is sometimes mistakenly thought of as an objective condition that must be escaped. At a talk in California, Lama Yeshe related the following story about a servant of a highly revered lama.

One day this servant began wearing a monk's robe. When sent on an errand to another lama, the lama questioned the servant about his spiritual progress. The servant answered that he had just transcended samsara. The lama was very inquisitive and begged him to reveal the method that allowed him to gain such a high level of attainment. The servant replied casually that he simply took off his layman's clothes.

Changing our physical status (monk's clothes or monastery existence) does not remove us from the wheel of death and birth and the karmic prison within the mind.

◇

Chöd
Meditation

To enhance renunciation, Tantric yogis perform a ritual called the *Chöd*, which literally means to cut. In this practice, the yogi cuts his or her attachment to the body and ego through a sacrificial offering of the body. The Chod was traditionally executed at

Figure 25. Vajra Varahi is one of the major Tantric dakinis and an expression of Vajra Yogini. She is used in meditation to awaken the Kundalini (Dumo Fire) and in the Chöd Ritual, which is based on the philosophy of the Prajna Paramita scriptures. She is sometimes referred to as the ''Diamond Sow'' and has a wild boar's head protruding from the right side of her head, symbolizing her integration of the unconscious aspects of the psyche rooted in the animal instincts. From the Avery Brundage Collection, Asian Art Museum of San Francisco, Golden Gate Park, San Francisco, CA. Reproduced here by permission.

twilight in remote or frightening places, such as cemeteries, and
most probably evolved from a pre-Buddhist rite of demon sacrifice. Tsultrim Allione, in her book *Women of Wisdom*, tells how the
offerings made at this time and in these places were thought to
appease the hungry ghosts so they wouldn't prey on innocent
people.[19] The meditation ritual is accompanied by a small drum,
bell, the human voice, and a trumpet made from a human thigh-
bone. The resulting sounds are very eerie, producing specific
vibrations in the body.

The Chöd practice is founded on the knowledge that
beneath the turmoil of the ego-self, the Buddha Mind exists in its
inherent bliss. If we can cut away the tendencies of the ego-self,
the Buddha Mind emerges naturally.[20]

Begin as usual with the Refuge meditation. When you have
settled into a tranquil state, visualize the central channel running
through the axis of your body from the top of the head to the floor
of the pelvis. This channel is hollow, about the size of your little
finger, and the translucent color of a blue flame. Within it at the
solar plexus is a small ball of light. As you breathe in, feel the vital
airs being drawn down the right and left channels (red and white
in color) from the nostrils to the first chakra. There the vital
winds enter the central channel and are forced upward during the
expiration. This fans the ball of light making it hotter and hotter
with each breath. Repeat the mantra OM AH HUNG; the first
two syllables while breathing in, and the last while exhaling.

On top of the ball of light, a fierce black goddess stands on
her left leg. (fig. 25 on page 152) She is naked except for a few
bone ornaments and a necklace of human skulls. Her genitals are
clearly visible, red, swollen, and moist. A wild boar's head pro-

---

[19]Tsultrim Allione, *Women of Wisdom* (London: Arkana, 1986), pp. 145–149.
[20]For more information about the Chod practice, refer to Khetsun Sangpo
Rinbochay, *Tantric Practice in Nying-Mapa* (Ithaca, NY: Snow Lion, 1982), pp.
161–166.

Figure 26. The Tibetan syllable *A* and the inverted seed mantra HAM. The Tibetan syllable *A* is related to the generative power of creation and visualized blazing hot in the root chakra in practices involved with the awakening of Kundalini. The seed mantra HAM is visualized upside down in the crown chakra. When the heat of the inner fire melts its bindu-like snow, its nectar drenches the meditator's body with bliss.

trudes from the right side of her head and her right leg is raised in
a dancing posture. In her raised right hand, poised to strike, she
holds a knife. Its crescent-shaped blade has a hooked end. This
knife was used to skin corpses in charnel-ground cemeteries in
India. The handle of her knife is a *vajra* (Tantric scepter) which
symbolizes the diamond-like energy of the Void.

Placed in front of her heart, her left hand holds a skullcap
filled with blood. The skullcap here represents her vagina. Like
the white semen of male deities, her blood is her spiritual
essence.

There is a staff that rests in the crook of her left elbow. The
trident on top of the staff stands for the transformation of the
three poisons of the mind: desire, aversion, and ignorance. Below
the trident there is a double vajra and three severed heads which
represent the three bodies (kayas) of the Buddha Mind. The first
skull is old and dry. It is the Dharmakaya, the transcendant Truth
Body. Though Void, it contains all potential. The second skull,
several weeks old, is the Sambogakaya. This is like an astral body
that Tantric deities use to manifest themselves to advanced yogis.
The third freshly cut head is the Nirmanakaya. This is a physical
embodiment of the Buddha Mind.

As you continue to shoot the vital winds up the central channel, the ball of light and the Black Dakini (Vajra Varahi, The
Diamond Sow) slowly rise up within the channel. When they pass
out the top of your head, your consciousness merges with her.
Gazing down on your former body, you see that it is very large.
As the Black Dakini, you reach down and cut off the top of your
head just above the eyes. You place this skullcap upside down on
three skulls as big as mountains in front of you. The ball of light,
which has turned into the flaming Tibetan syllable *a* burns
intensely beneath the skullcap. (See fig. 26 on page 154.) This
causes the skullcap to expand until it is large enough to place the
rest of the corpse in.

Now begin chopping up the rest of your body and place it piece by piece into the skull-cauldron. Pay attention to any feelings or memories that may arise as you carve up the different parts of your anatomy. As the body melts and then boils, visualize impurities rising to the surface and spilling over into the mouths of savage demons. At the same time heat rises in the form of steam to the cool white seed mantra HAM (fig. 26) which is suspended upside down over the cauldron. Like snow, its nectar melts to mix with the clarified essence of your corpse.

On the other side of the cauldron from you, the lineage of Tantric adepts and teachers sit on cushions in a semicircle. Bodhisattvas and the Dharma Protectors sit behind them. Beyond them are all your enemies and people to whom you owe debts. Above all of these in space, the Five Dhyani Buddhas and their consorts, arranged in a mandala, shine down on you. From the center of the four petaled mandala, the blue light of Vairocana's Pure Absolute Wisdom radiates. Below him, the white light of Aksobya's Mirror-Like Wisdom pours forth. To the left of the center, the yellow light of Ratnasambhava's Wisdom of Equality emanates. On the top, the red light of Amitabha's Discriminative Wisdom glows. And on the right of the center, the green light of Amoghasiddhi's All-Accomplishing Wisdom radiates.

Starting with the Five Buddhas and their consorts, see all the beings present partaking of the offering of nectar from the skullcap. Though they all imbibe the nectar in great amounts, it never diminishes. The five Buddha couples absorb the nectar through the light rays that shine from their bodies. The rest of the guests are served by numerous blue, white, yellow, red, and green dakinis who scoop nectar out of the large skull and offer it to them in their own skullcaps that they carry in their left hands.

When all have had their fill, you stir the simmering nectar and it vaporizes into great clouds. These rise on beautiful light beams and rainbows filling all of space. These clouds then rain down a light shower of blessings bestowing offerings on all sentient beings throughout all realms. All these beings are healed and all of their needs are fulfilled.

After this, everything dissolves into the Void. The last thing to merge into the Void is the flaming red letter *a*. Remain meditating in the sky-like emptiness of the Void as long as you enjoy it. Before coming out of meditation, mentally offer your most cherished possessions for the benefit of all sentient beings. Then feel how the Five Dhyani Buddhas and their consorts are pleased by your offerings. In return, they will bestow their spiritual powers on you to help remove all your remaining obscurations and non-virtues.

CHAPTER
SEVEN

◆

THE OCEAN
OF NECTAR

*T*he Sanskrit name for the sixth chakra is *Ajna*, meaning command from above. The Hindu diagram shows two lotus petals connected to a lunar disc, thought to be a reservoir for the nectar that drips down from the thousand petalled lotus on top of the head. The sixth chakra is often referred to as the ocean of nectar.

Within the lunar disc we find an inverted triangle, symbolic of the female genitals, with a lingam inside of it. There are two other chakras that contain this combination of the yoni and lingam—the root and heart chakras. It is in these three chakras that the power of Kundalini is concentrated. Also referred to as "knots," these three concentrations are associated with the physical, emotional, and mental bodies. See fig. 27 on page 160.

The sixth chakra is located in the center of the head. It is associated with the faculty of perception and related to the forebrain and cerebral cortex. These are in turn divided into the right and left hemispheres, and the two basic modes of perception— intuitive and rational, respectively.

The left hemisphere is predominantly involved with analytical, linear, and logical conceptual processes, such as mathematics. Generally thought of as the more masculine hemisphere, it governs the right side of the body.

The right hemisphere is primarily responsible for orientation in space—for instance, the recognition of complex visual patterns—and governs the left side of the body, which is thought of as the more receptive and feminine. It is involved with our aptitude for art and music, the recognition and expression of emotion, and the awareness of mystical or intuitive states.

The two primary subtle psychic channels, which originate in the sixth chakra and descend along the spinal column, can be associated with the functions of the left and right hemispheres of

Figure 27. The sixth chakra, Ajna, has two petals. These are joined by the Candra mandala associated with the ocean of nectar that drips down from the crown chakra and the six stages of samadhi or enlightenment. Within the inverted triangle inside the Candra mandala is the seed mantra OM, representing the innermost spirit associated with the pure Mind or Buddhi. Above the OM seed mantra is a nada and golden bindu, which, when added to the OM, create the mantra Pranava. This mantra expresses relationship between the Void and the generic factors of creation.

the brain. One of these channels is associated with the sun and represents the day force. The solar energies are considered to be centrifugal and move our consciousness toward rational aware-ness. The other channel is related to the moon and the forces of the night. Its centripetal movement takes us down into the unconscious mind where we experience the regenerative and uni-fying powers of the psyche.

In viewing the sixth chakra psychically, a front/back delinea-tion is perceived rather than a left/right split. The frontal portion, near the forehead and brow, correlates with the intellectual and assertive functions of consciousness. The portion near the center of the head is more receptive and intuitive.

People who live "in their heads"–always thinking and scheming–show a great deal of psychic energy in the area of the forehead. Actually, the energy often extends out in front of the brow as the forces of the intellect reach out to control the world. These people are caught up in their own thoughts and are out of touch with "what is." Not being receptive to input from the exter-nal or internal environment, these people seem to have a neurotic need to create and follow rigid conceptual patterns that give them a sense of security and knowing. Hence they are busy creating their own mental images of the world and imposing them on reality.

People who are focused in the center of the head are more receptive to emotional and intuitive information. Instead of trying to manipulate life to fit into preconceptions, these people intuit the inherent nature of the universe. Yet, without the balancing influence of the rational faculties, these types may have difficulty functioning within the rational parameters of our mundane world.

Ideally, intellect and intuition complement each other. In our modern world, however, over-emphasis on left-brain activity has upset this balance. When the right hemisphere of the brain is developed and used, latent intuitive abilities open new vistas and the "I" consciousness has glimpses of its essential unity with all that is. Psychic awareness is also stimulated.

The sixth chakra is sometimes called the third eye because of its potential for clairvoyance, the ability to perceive the subtle energies of non-physical realms. We all have this potential. In fact, in various ancient cultures these abilities were commonplace. Seeing auras, seeing the chakras, seeing into the future, seeing past lives or disincarnate beings, are all abilities that are available to us with an awakened sixth chakra.

Understanding the diversity of psychic senses makes it easy to see how two psychics may say very different things about the same person. Psychic awareness is more subjective than most psychics would like to admit. It is one thing to see something clearly, but another to interpret it. For instance, if you ask several people to study a painting and report what they see, you will get different descriptions. In psychic perception, information is translated via the belief systems and preconceptions of the psychic. Even information obtained via deep trance or mediumship, although eclipsing the intellect and conscious patterns, is filtered through the subconscious. The degree of distortion resulting from this filtering, of course, varies from person to person.

Filtering and coloring of the information received are examples of the dangers involved with using psychic powers before one is a "clear channel." Without consciously wishing to do so, some people use these abilities to manipulate others and to expand their own sense of importance. This is why most spiritual traditions strongly warn against concentrating on the development of psychic powers.

On a more mundane level, we also often misuse the power inherent in awareness. We desire to understand what is happening in our environment, either to gain control over it, or as a form of protection. By watching in order to control, we place ourselves outside of real life experience.

On the other hand, people with blocked sixth chakras do not want to see. Often they are rebelling against perspectives on life that were imposed either by their parents or the social structure. Or, because of traumatic and painful associations, they are refusing to see various aspects of human existence. It is not uncommon to find the physical vision of such people impaired by these attitudes.

Being a critic of life, not accepting it, wanting to change or control it, puts us at odds with life. If we could observe it from a neutral stance instead, we might be able to come to peace with the world. When we sit down at sunset and look over the fields and trees, watching the colors change in the sky, listening to the birds and feeling the calmness that surrounds us, we are not trying to control anything by being aware. Krishnamurti calls this "choiceless awareness."

Visualization may seem contradictory to cultivating choiceless awareness, but at higher levels of consciousness, there need not be a conflict between choiceless awareness and the creative use of mental faculties. Shakti Gawain, in *Creative Visualization*, uses a metaphor that might be helpful here. She correlates life to a river and says that most of us are hanging on to the bank because we are afraid to "go with the flow." Once we learn to trust that the river will carry us along safely, we can relax and flow down stream. Getting comfortable with this, we can then begin looking ahead to see how we might move with the current to best avoid obstacles.[1]

It is not what we see but how we see it that determines our experience. In an old Hindu story, a person seeing a rope lying on the ground in the darkness imagines it to be a snake. His subsequent behavior is completely based on this fantasy. In the same way, our experience of reality is almost entirely based on psycho-

---

[1]Shakti Gawain, *Creative Visualization* (Mill Valley, CA: Whatever Publishing, 1978), pp. 44

logical projection. We are caught in the illusions of the ego and its samsaric experience, and do not see the absolute nature of the world. Would it not, therefore, be beneficial to develop a more enlightened method of "visualizing" the world?

Can you picture yourself as a more relaxed and open person, flowing between the banks of the here-and-now while remaining connected to your source? Can you see yourself just being aware of and appreciating the beauty and mystery that unfolds, or observing the more distasteful scenery without reaction or identification, as you follow the meandering course of life? Can you visualize yourself as a Buddha? Abiding calmly in the Clear Light, which you perceive shining through the flux of ephemeral phenomena, you are conjoined with the "suchness" of life and the Bliss and Compassion pouring forth from the heart of the Void.

◇

The Mind and
the Mental
Body

When we are aware of something, it is the mind that makes it conscious and gives it meaning. The mind, however, is not consciousness. It is a vehicle of consciousness and, like the body, the mind has form and functions. It can be developed and used properly, or it can be abused and become unhealthy.

The mind may also be compared to a mirror. Through it we do not know things themselves, but only their effects produced in the mind. This mirroring is subject to distortion. Our experience of the world is a result of the functions of our minds. We are therefore victims of its structure, conceptual patterns, and modes of operation.

Before we look at how the Buddhists view the mind, let's examine its various facets by considering the anatomy of the mental body and its relationship to the nervous system and brain. Modern science has been frustrated in attempting to understand thought and consciousness because the source of these phenomena is in the mental body, not in the electro-chemical processes of nerve tissue. I'd like to suggest that the nervous system is merely the "wiring" which carries signals to and from the physical organs of consciousness. Rather than the mind being in the physical body or brain, the body and brain actually exist within the mind, or the mental body, which, like the astral body but on a higher frequency, surrounds the physical body.

The brain and nervous system are a magnificant bio-computer whose signaling system is both electrical and chemical. The various functions of the brain are operated by a complicated network of neurons. Almost every neuron receives input from many hundred, sometimes thousands, of other neurons. The entire central nervous system (brain and spinal cord) consists of billions of neurons. Sensory information acts as input data into the bio-computer, which in turn processes the data and then sends signals out to motor neurons to operate muscles and glands. J. H. Walle, in his article "The Organization of the Brain," claims that this central bio-computer is composed of about 99.98 percent of the brain's neurons.[2]

The internal functions of this bio-computer are still hidden to the probing eye of modern science. What integrates and regulates the complex operations of this incredible bio-computer? Could it be the mental body via the etheric body and chakras?

Though admittedly speculative, here are some working hypotheses that I have developed in my healing work. When I clairvoyantly view the mental body, it appears like a large dome,

---

[2]J. H. Walle and N. & M. Feirtag, "The Organization of the Brain," in *Scientific American*, Sept. 1979, Vol. 241, p. 97.

with a radius of nine to twenty feet, surrounding the physical body. The size and brilliance of the mental body is apparently related to the development of mental faculties. A central core, about a foot in diameter, extends from the top to the bottom through its axis. Like the central nervous system, this core functions as a communications exchange. It is linked to memory banks that radiate out from it, and it records, analyzes, and responds to various internal and external stimuli. Specific parts of the mental body relate to locations in the astral, etheric and physical bodies, which are all integrated through the multidimensional functions of the chakras. Information related to any particular aspect of the body-mind is stored in the corresponding area of the mental body.

The analyzing function automatically scans all of the information contained in the mental body as it records and responds to stimuli. This process may not always be logical or even beneficial, as a basic understanding of the psychological phenomena of association readily demonstrates. The association process is primarily mechanical and, like a computer, the capabilities and output are dependent on the nature of its programming.

In the brain, learning and memory are related to repeated use of certain neurological pathways. Similarly, in the mental body, preferred or strong impressions and associated patterns constitute learned and perpetuated mental dispositions. These structured responses, attitudes, and conceptual frameworks are relatively concrete, as far as the substance of the mental plane is concerned.

Our sense of identity and our individual constructs of reality are built into these mental structures. Although useful, the main difficulty with these constructs is that they usually prevent us from expanding the horizons of our awareness. Like any scanning device, the ego records only that input which can be related to the information already stored in the memory banks. Foreign experiences enter the mental body and find no program or pattern with which they can be associated. They are not mirrored in the mind and cannot be accepted in the existing reality construct, and thus they remain unintelligible. Such experiences either create confusion or are ignored completely, especially when they threaten existing conceptual realities.

To round out our model of the mind, let's turn to the phenomenology of it developed by the Buddhists. The early Buddhists recorded their insight into the nature of the mind in writings called the Abhidharma. The Abhidharma includes sense perceptions, emotions, complex mental processes, trance and mystical states of consciousness.

Phenomenal reality is conceived by the Buddhist to be inseparable from the subjective flow of sensations, perceptions, emotions, and mental activities. The mind is continually synthesizing images and concepts which it believes is reality. The Abhidharma examines how the mind does this and what elements it uses to construct this "reality."

The mental elements used by the mind are best thought of as events rather than things. They are forces or tendencies in the mind, called *sarvantranga* in Sanskrit—literally "going everywhere." There are five essential mental elements which are intimately related to the five Wisdom Energies of the Dhyani Buddhas.

The first of these five elements is called *sparsa*, to have rapport or contact. Sparsa describes the relationship between objects, our sense organs, and the consciousness that is aware of the experience. Only the combination of all three of these factors creates our "real" experience because neither the external object, nor the observer can be experienced independently. This unified field, or gestalt appreciation or existence means that not only do objects affect us, but our perception of them also affects them. Modern physics has recently discovered this ancient Buddhist principle.

The mental event that follows rapport with an object is *vedana*, or feeling-tone. It is related to second chakra feeling-judgments. Feeling-judgments create subjective values for acceptance or avoidance of experiences. These responses are usually programmed from prior experiences of pleasure or pain. They may also be influenced by past and present social conditioning. As the intensity of feeling increases, it will turn into an effect, shifting and directing the body-mind into appropriate action.

The third mental process makes sense out of incoming data. This process is called *samjna*. The main aspect of samjna is to know by association, and it is closely related to the ego function and therefore socialization. Any thought in the mind implies someone who is doing the thinking. This conceptualizing function of the mind can be used on any level of experience, from the most mundane to the most sublime.

Prior to action, a mental process takes place to galvanize the mind. This dynamic function is called *cetana*, translated as volition. However subtle it might be, when the mind settles on an object or thought, it is an act of volition—there has been a decision to focus on the object of awareness. There is some reason or motive behind what we pay attention to. The Buddhists also refer to this cetana force as the "monkey mind" because it is ceaselessly jumping from one thing to another. By now you are well aware of this wandering cetana force. As you have attempted to do the meditations in earlier chapters, you observed the mind's tendency to be drawn to one idea or memory after another, and to be affected by the awareness of sensory input. The mind actually seems to have a mind of its own! This is the cetana force.

Complementary to the cetana force is *manaskara*, translated to mean concentration, or application. The mind runs wild unless it is harnessed. There are two aspects to this concentrating force. First is *samadhi*, the ability to stablize the mind on a single object of thought, and second, *prajna*, the ability to have precise or heightened awareness.

Samadhi is normally associated with a deep state of meditation, yet it can also denote a relaxed but intense state of concentration. This state dissolves any separation between ourselves and any activity that we might be engaged in. When an artist is painting, for example, he or she is completely absorbed in the work. In this state of at-one-ment with what we are doing, all five of the mental processes are operating in harmony.

Prajna is a very revered mental element. It offers us the ability to have a precise comprehension of all the other mental events. It is considered to be the mother of wisdom. It also has two qualities; the first is discriminative, enabling us to articulate the other mental events. The second quality is one of appreciation. Not only can we be very clear in our perception of experiences, but we can appreciate the unique qualities inherent in their composition as they are formed in the matrix of our mental events. There is a certain beauty in the intermingling of awareness with this mysterious flow of events. And there is a lightheartedness and twinkle in the eye when this aspect of wisdom smiles from within us.

Walt Anderson, in *Open Secrets*, shares a metaphor that he heard from a Buddhist teacher. The mind can be compared to a flock of birds that moves in a formation while constantly changing its shape and direction. When we begin watching the mind, it shifts back and forth like these birds. Sometimes we are the observer, and sometimes we are the flock of birds. When we learn how to be both at the same time we have developed prajna, the "power of simultaneous awareness" as it is sometimes called.[3]

When we study the events of the mind, we become aware of its unceasing movement, a kaleidoscope of images composed of the intricate patterns of mental processes, swiftly changing preconceptions, feeling judgments, memories, associations, and so on. Through self-observation we begin to see how many of our

---

[3]Walt Anderson, *Open Secrets* (New York: Penguin, 1979), p. 50.

problems in life stem from misinterpretation, projection, desire, and aversion. All these arise in the processes of mental events, none of which are involved with Absolute Reality.

$$\Diamond$$

The Buddha Mind

It is said that when the Buddha reached Enlightenment, he was asked what he had attained. He replied with a laugh and said, "nothing."

In deep meditation, the mind becomes concentrated and observant and we can see how all mental phenomena are empty processes. There is no "self" to be found in them. When we have a profound realization of the emptiness of the self, and the emptiness of all phenomena, it vanquishes our desire to cling to any object or mental condition.

In the last section I said the mind is like a mirror, yet if we search for this mirror we cannot find it. It is transparent, clear, lucid awareness that allows things to be reflected in it, but when the object is removed the mind itself is invisible. The absolute nature of the Mind can be experienced directly as the ultimate state of consciousness but it cannot be conceptualized or intellectually understood. The Buddhists refer to it as the *Dharmakaya*, which means the body of truth, or the formless body of the Buddha (the personification of the Enlightened Mind).

Meditation ultimately proceeds to the condition of "no mind," a state beyond the duality inherent in normal mental activities, to experience the naked lucidity of the Enlightened Mind. There are four basic methods to facilitate the high level of concentration needed for this endeavor. These are the use of mantra, visualization, breath, and posture.

The word *mantra* comes from the Sanskrit noun *manas*, meaning mind, and the verbal root *tra*, to protect. Mantras protect the mind from wayward thoughts. Mantras are cosmic forces embodied in the structure of sound. Every mantra contains vibrations with specific powers. The repetition of a mantra produces certain rhythms and patterns of psychic energy in the subtle bodies that release blockages and open pathways for the Kundalini energy.

Closely related to mantras are yantras, which embody cosmic forces in geometric or circular diagrams. Each yantra makes visible the patterns of force heard in the mantra. See fig. 28. Visualization of yantras concentrate and focus the mind in meditation. Yantras, also called mandalas, are composed of either abstract graphic configurations or illustrations of deities arranged into geo-

Figure 28. The Shri Yantra represents the complete cosmos created by the balance of male and female principles, here symbolized by the various combinations of upward and downward pointing triangles.

metric compositions. To identify wholly with the yantra is to realize, or release, the inherent forces that each form denotes.

Yantras, or mandalas, are not unique to the Tantric tradition, they are readily associated with archetypal projections of transpersonal dimensions of the psyche found throughout the world. Jung realized that his patients spontaneously drew and dreamed mandala/yantra-like patterns, especially when all the making or healing functions of the Self were active. He also noted that these expressions of the Self are evident in many diverse cultures through the course of history.

Closely associated with the intoning of mantras and the visualization of yantras and deities is the use of specific body postures, called *mudras*. Mudras are functionally related to certain states of consciousness and the movement of psychic energies through the body. While some of these hand and body gestures are symbolic, it is not uncommon for people to find their bodies moving spontaneously into specific mudras while experiencing the awakening of spiritual forces. Anyone who has experienced this will quickly inform you that the magnetic-like forces that shape the body during these intense encounters with powerful psychic energies are not symbolic gestures. They are literal expressions of these forces.

A common meditation mudra is the full lotus or vajra-position, the mudra of the Dhyani Buddha Varicona. The hands lie on top of one another in the lap. For a man, the right on top of the left. For a woman the left hand is on the top. The legs are folded so the soles of the feet face upward. In this position, energy recirculates throughout the body, rather than being lost through the limbs. The position is very stable and the spine is perfectly erect allowing a free flow of the vital airs through the main energy channels along the spine. This mudra instills peace and tranquility and represents a harmonious balance of energies.

Breathing exercises, called *pranayama* in Sanskrit, are also used to still and focus the mind. The breath is directly related to emotional and mental states. When we are fearful or angry, the breath is rapid. When startled or when concentrating, breath may stop. Conversely, the breath can be used to control or alter emotional-mental states. A slow, deep, and regular breathing pattern has a very calming and stilling effect on the body-mind. Some forms of meditation rely almost exclusively on this simple method. By using the breath as an object of concentration, the mind is stilled and led into meditation. More complicated breathing techniques are used in conjunction with elaborate visualizations to circulate the vital airs (breath) and to draw them into the central channel.

The Sanskrit word *prana* is often translated as simply breath. It actually connotes a rarified life force that pervades and sustains all manifested forms. *Ayama* means extension or restraint. Pranayama, therefore, means extension or restraint of the life force so that the body-mind may be vitalized to its highest potential.

A basic phenomenon associated with the nervous system is important here. Merely directing attention to a specific area of the body will stimulate the nervous system in that region. The intense concentration involved in the practice of meditation upon the chakras and the special breathing exercises of Tantra stimulate the nervous system. The location of the chakras in the etheric body coincide with the major nerve ganglia along the spine. The size of the spinal cord, this channel can transmit a tremendous neurological charge. Because repeated concentration on the chakras activates neurological pathways, the ability and predilection of the spinal cord to propagate electrical charges of great magnitude is increased.

Tantra maintains that some of the major psychic channels in the etheric body are subtle counterparts of the nervous system. Prana is said to flow through these channels. An increased flow of electrical current is, therefore, the result of the prana moving through the subtle channels of the etheric body. As we open these channels and learn to direct the pranic force through them, we gradually alter the anatomy and capacity of both the subtle and physical bodies.

Prana is believed to enter the physical body through the chakras of the etheric body. Tantric doctrine delineates five distinct classifications of vital airs, corresponding to the modification of prana according to its location and function in the chakras. Two of these represent the main focus of breathing techniques. Apana, the downward breath, is located in the first chakra, and prana, the principal vital air, is related to the heart center. Prana is manipulated to flow downward, vitalizing the latent primordial power of Kundalini and causing apana to rise. By reversing their usual path and bringing them together in the third chakra, a great deal of psychic heat is generated. This inner fire is used to open the central channel.

Among the many mandalas and yantras in Tantra, the body-mind is the most important. Composing it are the rhythms and forces that move through all creation. It is, therefore, a potent symbol of the cosmos. Unleashing and harmonizing the flow of the life force through the chakras reveals its powers and secrets. Through a precise use of body posture, mantra, breath control and visualization, we can focus and purify the body-mind, creating suitable conditions for the Clear Light of the Buddha-Mind to flood into the central channel and pour into our awareness like sunlight into a dark room.

$$\Diamond$$

Deity Yoga

Deity yoga is a very powerful technique to transform the finite mind into the Buddha Mind. This aspect of Tantra is so effective that it is said to lead us to enlightenment in one lifetime. In order

to practice it correctly we need first to master the three principles: (1) renunciation, the determination to let go of the ego
identity and its world view; (2) compassion, the ardent desire to
become a Buddha for the sake of all sentient beings; and (3) the
correct view, the profound awareness that all phenomena are
temporal and devoid of inherent existence. We have already discussed the first two, let's consider now the third.

The Sanskrit word for the Void (*Shunyata*) literally means
emptiness, but it has a more subtle connotation when used in
Buddhist philosophy. The concept of voidness relates to the
experience, realized in meditation, that there is no abiding principle in things. There is no independent and irreducible stuff from
which things are made, and therefore nothing exists of and by
itself. All things are composed of other temporal elements, continually arising, combining, and passing away, from and into the
great no-thingness of the Void.

When we look at the physical world, we normally see the
delimited forms of objects, rather than the field in which they
appear. In the same way, thoughts predominate in the mind, and
the space in which they occur is ignored. The Void is like the
negative space in which things exist. Yet, far from being an empty
or negative state, the Void is a very positive state, one containing
infinite potential. This openness is omnipresent and presupposed
by every object. All things take form out of it and exist only in
relationship to it.

The Void is the ultimate and formless Reality. It is an inde-
finable mystery in which the ceaseless flow of phenomenal reality
exists. To realize It as one's true nature is to become a Buddha, to
not realize It is to remain in the state of cyclic existence and
illusion.

Through a heightened state of awareness, the Void is experienced as pure consciousness. There is a tremendous sense of
freedom in this state, a feeling of having gone beyond. The mind's
essential nature is like space; it is all pervasive. In his Mahamudra

instruction, the Mahasiddhi yogi Tilopa tells us to be still and stay relaxed, to be quiet and let sound reverberate as a hollow echo. When we are able to keep the mind silent, then we will see the ending of all worlds. Compassion and renunciation are the gate and path of Tibetan Tantra, profound meditation on the Void is the abode of calm abiding.

Through Deity yoga we are joined to the mind of the deity who dwells in this calm abode. To begin we must learn how to distill the mind's five essential aggregates (skandhas). The Sanskrit word *skandha* means to shoulder, or hold up. As we learned in the study of the Abhidharma, the five skandhas (mental elements) support the illusions of our ego reality. When these elements of the mind are transformed back into their pristine nature, the obscurations of the finite mind are cleansed from the mirror-like clarity of the Buddha Mind.

The Sanskrit verb *nirva* means literally "to blow out." The connotation when used in Tantra refers to a fire going out because the fuel has been exhausted. When the five skandhas are transmuted, there is no more fuel for the ego-mind. Consciousness is then liberated from the defilements that have obscured its essential voidness. In Sanskrit, this state of consciousness is called *jnana*.

Both jnana and prajna contain the root *jna*, which signifies the cognitive potentials of consciousness. The prefix *pra* means to heighten or intensify. Therefore prajna refers to an enhancement of the cognitive faculties. Consciousness is thus purged of obscurations, and the diamond-like clarity of the Void is perceived. Jnana refers to the primordial nature of the Buddha Mind. Whereas the Void is an object perceived by the prajna quality, jnana is pre-existent to a subject-object duality. Jnana is the nondual suchness of pristine Void Awareness personified in Vajradhara, the Adhibuddha.

Vajradhara is worshipped as the "root guru" because He is the form that the Buddha Mind assumes to teach Tantra. Prajnaparamita, consort to Vajradhara, represents cognition in its most sublime state (prajna) experiencing Transcendent Wisdom (paramita). She personifies the Wisdom of the Yonder Shore, the awareness that transports us across the ocean of cyclic existence.

A daily meditation ritual, called the *guru puja*, is practiced to transform yourself into the exalted state of an embodiment of Vajradhara and Prajnaparamita. This is one example of Deity yoga. There are a number of more involved higher Buddhist Tantric methods based on a particular deity and their host of attendants. Such deities as Hevajra, Chakrasambhara, Guhyasamaja, and Kalachakra all have their own mandalas and different methods of working with, and even descriptions of, the chakras and subtle channels.

The differences in the various Tantric systems can most probably be accounted for by the distance in time and location that separates them. Just as the universal motifs found in world mythology display individual characteristics in various cultures, the archetypal elements in Tantric rituals appear in unique expression in different sects.

Because of the mythic and symbolic nature of these systems, it is not appropriate to make a judgment about which of them is more correct, or even desirable. Unless you are being guided by a teacher of a particular method, it is best to approach these matters with an open mind. Thus it has been my intention to present basic principles and encourage you to be alert to your own intuition. For example, my own experiences with the awakening of the Inner Fire did not conform to the "dogma" of the teachings into which I was initiated.

The Buddhists say that placing the mind in higher Tantric practices of Deity yoga without first preparing it is like dropping a stone in water; it will not absorb anything. Traditionally, in addition to the Refuge, Insight, Vajrasattva, and Chöd meditations, a student also performs 100,000 prostrations and mandala offerings to the root guru Vajradhara and entire lineage of Buddhist teachers. The value of these preliminary practices cannot be stressed too much. They are the prime reason the Tantric method is so effective.

The higher Tantric practices contain two stages: the generation stage in which we imagine the movement of vital airs through channels, and ourselves as the deity in its mandala; and the stage of completion where the vital airs actually enter and dissolve in the central channel and we become a literal incarnation of the deity.

Daniel Cozort, in *Highest Yoga Tantra*, elaborates the importance of "divine pride" in the generation stage. This is like a form of self-hypnosis in which we believe, and act as if, we are the meditational deity. By cultivating this divine self-image, not only in meditation but throughout all the activities of each day, we are protected from our ordinary perception of the world. The "I" created in this Deity yoga is based on our realization of emptiness and is a powerful antidote to normal illusions of the ego self.[4]

When the vital airs enter the central channel, both the pressure of inhalation and exhalation and the amount of air moving through each nostril are equal. At more advanced levels of practice, breathing gets slower and eventually appears to stop. Along with the manipulation of vital airs, we are also instructed to use sexual union (with either a literal or visualized consort) in order to join its bliss with our contemplation on emptiness. The union of these two produces the necessary conditions in which the Buddha Mind is realized.

The meditation example that follows is a composite of higher Tantric practices, including a brief guru puja to Vajradhara, the Four Tantric Empowerments, a breathing technique called Vase Breathing, visualization of the vital airs and subtle energy channels, work with the Inner Fire, and a condensed form of the Shri Chakrasambhara Tantra. It should be noted that these different

---

[4]Daniel Cozort, *Highest Yoga Tantra* (Ithaca, NY: Snow Lion, 1986), p. 117.

practices are not traditionally combined in this way. This simulation merely illustrates the complex elements involved in the higher Tantric methods.

◇

Shri Chakrasambhara Tantra

Chakrasambhara is a wrathful expression of Vajradhara used in a meditation ritual to gain initiation into the Great Bliss. *Sambhara* literally means a collection or a vow. The Chakrasambhara Mandala (which includes some sixty-two deities) represents the Highest Bliss. Because Shri Chakrasambhara Tantra has the power to free us from the wheel of cyclic existence, it takes place in a vast cremation ground which symbolizes the end of worldly existence. This Tantra is said to have been passed from Vajradhara to the celestial guru and Bodhisattva Vajrapani, who in turn gave it to the Indian Buddhist saint Saraha. It has been passed from teacher to teacher ever since those ancient times, including such venerated teachers as Tilopa and Naropa.

• • •

In the vast expanse of the sky, there is a golden throne supported by eight lions (symbolizing fearlessness and the conquest of all obnoxious powers). On this throne is a pure white lotus (undefilement by evil), in which the moon and sun rest like cushions (respectively, the dispersal of all darkness of spiritual ignorance, and the emanation of the light of transcending awareness). Seated here in full lotus position, Vajradhara holds the scepter and bell (wisdom and compassion) in his left and right

Figure 29. Vajradhara is considered to be the Supreme Buddha (Adibuddha) by two of the major sects of Tibetan Buddhism. He is worshipped as the Root Guru and the form that the Buddha-Mind assumes to transmit the Tantric teachings. Contemporary painting by Äge Delbanco reproduced by permission of the artist.

hands, which are crossed in front of his heart. His body is the blue of the midnight sky and is adorned with jewels and heavenly silk. He is resplendent with light and enhaloed by the five-colored rainbow of the Dhyani Buddhas gone to Bliss. (See fig. 29.)

Clustered below Vajradhara are all the gurus that have been the disciples of the Root Guru Vajradhara. To the left is Shakyamuni Buddha in the form that he appears in the Refuge meditation. On top of Vajradhara sits Prajnaparamita (fig. 30 on page 182). Her body is the color of the clear blue day sky. Her hands meet in front of her heart in the mudra of "link of increase," meaning coronation or marriage of above and below. A lotus stem, held in her left hand, rises up to support a sacred book containing the teachings on the Void. To the right of Vajradhara are the Bodhisattvas Tara (fig. 31 on page 184), and Avalokitesvara who represent the entire community of Buddhist practitioners.

The lineage of enlightened teachers are acknowledged and asked for their blessings and assistance. Then they dissolve into the Root Guru, Vajradhara, who incorporates them all. Then Shakyamuni, Parajnaparamita, Avalokitesvara, and Tara dissolve into Vajradhara. You can pray in your own words to the root guru to bless your mindstream so that it can be cleansed of its defilements. Traditional prayers help in developing the Great Compassion, heartfelt renunciation, and the correct view of voidness. Finally, permission to practice the two Tantric stages of generation and completion would be asked for.

Vajradhara would then bestow the four Tantric empowerments on you. From the white OM in his sixth chakra, light pours into the small drop of light in the central channel in your own sixth chakra. The Vase Initiation is granted, cleansing and correcting the subtle energy channels in your body. This empowers you to perform the developmental stages of higher Tantric practices, and plants the seed that will grow into an Emanation Body of a Buddha (Nirmanakaya). Receiving this empowerment makes

Figure 30. Prajna Paramita is the deification of the Buddhist scripture
of the same name. She embodies Transcendent Wisdom and is
therefore considered the ''Mother of all the Buddhas.'' Some sects of
Tibetan Buddhism identify her as the consort of Vajradhara, the
Supreme Buddha. From the Avery Brundage Collection, Asian Art
Museum of San Francisco, Golden Gate Park, San Francisco, CA.
Reproduced here by permission.

you reflect on the importance and creative potential of your physical body. When purified, it will be the vehicle of the Buddha Mind.

Next, the red light from the AH in his throat chakras beams into and activates the drop of light in your own throat chakra (in the central channel). The vital airs, which among other things generate speech, are purified by this – the Secret Initiation. This empowers you to use mantra correctly so you can meditate on the body's subtle energy systems, and plants the seed for the development of an Illusory Body of a Buddha (Sambhogakaya). This body is more permanent than your present temporal form; it will survive physical death. This empowerment also transforms your modes of communication, internal and external. Just as some people mindlessly talk about essentially meaningless things, your own mind is constantly chattering. The use of mantra is communication on a different level. It creates a rapport with higher truths and protects your mind from its habitual neurotic rambling.

Blue light then shines from the HUM in Vajradhara's heart chakra into your heart chakra. The drop of light there in the central channel is activated as you receive the Wisdom Empowerment. This enables you to engage in the practice of union of nondual suchness, and plants the seeds for the Truth Body of a Buddha (the Dharmakaya). People normally create concepts and mental images to represent or label events, and then mistake these labels and images for the reality they represent. These "wrong views," and the predilection to create them, is interrupted by the Vajra Mind through this empowerment. In addition, the winds that move through the subtle channels are purified. The transformation of worldly desires into the Great Bliss is potentized and you become capable of being a vessel for this bliss.

The Word Empowerment integrates the other three initiations. Hence you would visualize the white, red, and blue rays shining into your higher three chakras. This purifies the underly-

Figure 31. Tara is one of the most popular goddesses of Tibet; there are twenty-one different expressions of her. Legend says that Tara was born from a tear that fell from the eye of the Buddha of Compassion (Avalokiteshvara) when he looked down on humanity and experienced all their suffering. With the innocence and purity of a 16-year-old girl, Tara vowed to liberate all sentient beings. Her Tibetan name, Dolma, means deliveress. From the Thanka collection of Sergei Diakoff, reproduced here by permission.

ing basis for all obstructions to omniscience. You are thus transformed into a vessel for the Great Perfection. When this initiation
is conducted by a lama, you are given permission to practice
Mahamudra (to be discussed in the next chapter).

Vajradhara is the personification of the underlying Void unity
from which the five Wisdom-Energies emanate. Through guru
yoga, you are joining your body, speech, and mind with him in
order to merge into his Beingness.[5] At this point, you would
visualize yourself transforming into Vajradhara. As your mind
enters one-pointed concentration on the Void, you would dissolve
into the Clear Light.

When you could no longer remain in this delicate balance of
thoughtlessness, your mind would appear in the form of a crescent moon, white tinged with red. Below this in space, visualize a
sun disc in the center of an eight-petalled lotus. There is another
circle outside of this; it has eight blue lotus petals and is the
Mandala of the Mind. Outside of this, another circle contains
eight red lotus petals, the Mandala of Speech. Around this is the
white eight-petalled Mandala of the Body.

Enshrining all of this is a vast square temple (fig. 32 on page
186). Its walls are made of five precious materials: at ground
level, a black substance like onyx, on top of this white conch
shells, next gold, then rubies, and finally emeralds. A Chinese-
style roof rests on these. Each wall has an entrance and a small
porch supported by pillars. A four-tiered cornice, colored blue at
the east gate, green at the north, red on the west, and yellow on
the south, rests on top of these pillars. Surrounding the temple is
a wall of flames, the blazing fire of Transcendental Wisdom.

---

[5]For more information about guru yoga and the Four Tantric Empowerments,
refer to *The Mahamudra: Eliminating the Darkness of Ignorance*, by the Ninth
Karmapa, Wang-Ch'ug Dorje, translated and edited by Alexander Berzin
(Dharamsala, India: Library of Tibetan Works and Archives, 1978), pp.
17–20.

Figure 32. Chakrasambhara Mandala. This is the Mandala visualized in the Chakrasambhara Tantra, one of the more esoteric and higher Tantric practices. It shows the central eight-petalled lotus, the four dakinis on its cardinal points, and within it the chief devatas, Chakrasambhara and Vajra Yogini. Outside of this are the three mandalas of the body, speech, and mind. Enshrining this is a temple located among eight cremation grounds. From the Avery Brundage Collection, Asian Art Museum of San Francisco, Golden Gate Park, San Francisco, CA. Used by permission.

Radiating out beyond this there are eight Great Cremation Grounds. Each of these has a large tree, a river, a fire, a stupa, and a large cloud hovers over each cremation ground. This huge cemetery exists on top of Mount Meru, the highest imaginable place in the world.

The following devatas abide in the eight cemeteries: yellow Indra on his elephant holding a thunderbolt, yellow Yaksha on a horse holding a mace, white Varuna on Makara with his nose, blue Yama on a buffalo holding a lance, red Agni with four arms riding a goat, black Rakshasa holding a sword and skull and mounted on a revived corpse, green Marut holding a banner and riding a deer, and white Vang-Dan on a bull with a three-pointed thunderbolt. All of these devatas are accompanied by their consorts and are gazing toward you, appearing now as the chief Devata in the center of the concentric circles of the four-fold mandala.

As Chakrasambhara (fig. 33 on page 188), you would visualize your body as translucent deep sky blue and smeared with ashes from the cremation grounds. You would have one face and two arms crossed in front of your heart embracing your consort, Vajra Yogini. (Chakrasambhara also appears with sixteen arms and four faces.) In your hands you hold a vajra scepter and a bell. To signify that you have acquired the fullest measure of merits, your hair is tied in a knot on top of your head. This is adorned with a gem that grants all wishes to those who pray to you. A crescent moon rests on the left side of the knot; it shows that you have attained the highest level of consciousness. On top of the knot, there is a multicolored four-pronged vajra scepter that denotes that your actions serve all beings. You also wear a crown of five dry skulls because you have perfected the five wisdoms of the Dhyani Buddhas. A necklace of fifty freshly severed heads represents the letters of the sacred alphabet. To show that the demon goddess of desire has been overcome, you frown and display your fangs. You also wear a loose fitting tiger skin to

Figure 33. Chakrasambhara and Vajra Yogini. Chakrasambhara is a wrathful form of the Adibuddha, Vajradhara, used in an advanced Tantric method. His consort, Vajra Yogini, is one of the primary goddesses of Tibetan Tantra. She is associated with the emptiness that is the matrix from which creation emerges, and is therefore considered to be the "Mother of Creation." Contemporary painting by Äge Delbanco reproduced here by permission of the artist.

demonstrate your heroic disregard for the belief in the reality of matter and mind.

You are serious, energetic, stern, and awe inspiring, yet you are compassionate and ever ready to save erring souls overpowered by passions and wayward thoughts. To show that you still exist in the world of sentient beings, you tread with outstretched right leg on the emaciated red body of the goddess of time. Your bent left leg stands on a black figure to remind all beings to avoid extreme doctrines, such as the doctrine that Nirvana is the sole reality.

Your body is virile and graceful as you embrace Vajra Yogini. She is red, the color of intense passion and love, because she loves all beings. She clings to you fervently, yet she is so responsive to your slightest movement that you can hardly feel her touch. She has two arms; the left embraces you and holds a skullcap filled with her blood. She thus confers her essence— Supreme Bliss. Her right hand holds the vajra knife with which she cuts away all discursive thoughts and obscuring desires. To show that she has untied the knot that holds all things as they appear, her hair hangs long and free. She is naked, exposing the truth of her being free from all veils of desire and erroneous concepts. She has three eyes, is crowned with five dried skulls, and wears five bone ornaments. Her legs are wrapped around your upper thighs. Her sexual union with you causes the two of you to be inseparable from the oneness of Supreme Wisdom and Bliss.

On the four lotus petals of the four cardinal directions of the innermost mandala around you, four youthful naked Dakinis with long tusseled hair stand with their right legs stretched out. Each has one face, three eyes, crowns of five dried skulls, necklaces of fifty dried heads, and fangs protruding from sensual smiles. In their two right hands they hold a curved knife and small double-sided drum. In their left hands they hold a skullcap and staff. Each Dakini has a white OM on a moon disc at her brow, a red

AH on a lotus at her throat, and blue HUM on a sun disc at her heart. The Black Dakini stands on the eastern petal, the green Dakini stands on the northern petal, the red Dakini is on the western petal, and on the southern petal is the yellow Dakini.

On the lotus petals of the four intervening points of the compass are four urns made of precious metals. These are filled with the waters of wisdom. On top of these are skulls filled with the five nectars, thus making the Chakra (wheel) of Great Bliss.

Beyond this are the three mandalas of the mind, speech, and body. On each of the eight lotus petals in all the mandalas, gods and goddesses embrace one another. The male deities have four arms. Two of the hands hold a vajra scepter and bell crossed behind the backs of their consorts whom they are embracing. Their other right hand holds a drum and the left hand holds a staff. The female deities all resemble Vajra Yogini in ornament and posture. All these gods and goddesses are filled with Great Bliss.

The three outer mandalas represent the three bodies of the Buddha Mind. The outermost white mandala is the Manifestation Body. The red mandala of speech is the Emanation Body. And the inner blue mandala of the mind is the Truth Body. All of the divine couples inhabiting these mandalas represent things that happen on the Path of Liberation, such as helpful impulses and the states arrived at by their means.

Having created a vivid image of the three mandalas and their residing deities, you would repeat the mantra OM AH HUM. As you chant each syllable, the couples of its respective mandala are activated. When chanting OM, concentrate on the outer mandala of the body. When chanting AH, focus on the red mandala of speech. When chanting HUM, be aware of the blue mandala of the mind.

Repeat this process three times. At the end of each repetition, concentrate on the four dakinis of the central mandala, and the embrace of your consort. The bliss generated by the couples in the outer mandalas would be focused within you and your consort. This causes the red *a* in your first chakra to heat up and buzz. Its heat rises to melt the point of light in the Thig-Le in the head. It then begins to hum and drip nectar. The dripping white nectar mixes with the rising red heat in the heart chakra.

In Tantra it is thought that bliss is generated in the lower end of the central channel during sexual intercourse by the heating of letter *a* there. As this heat rises up the central channel, it melts the upside down HAM in the head center. The nectar from it drips down to produce pleasurable sexual feelings.

The central channel, which runs up through all the "chakra-wheels" like an axle, transparent blue (some sources describe it as clear tinged with red) and the size of your little finger, is vividly pictured. At its lowest end (the first chakra) the seed-syllable *a* (fig. 26 on page 154) is visualized, fine as a hair, an inch high, and red hot like an incandescent filament. This *a* is mysteriously alive with vital energy and makes a sound like a tight string being vibrated by the wind.

At the other end of the central channel is the sixth chakra; the seed-syllable HAM (fig. 26) is visualized, white like the moon, and filled with the nectar of the Bodhicitta. It makes a humming sound like a swarm of bees.

To increase the heat of the *a*, a breathing technique called Vase Breathing is used. During the inhale, air is visualized coming in the nostrils and filling up the right and left channels as if they were balloons. After completing the inhale, the abdomen is extended (making the body appear like a vase) while the air is swallowed and forced downward. This pushes the air out of the two channels into the central channel at its lower end. The sphincter muscle is then contracted to trap the air in the central channel and force it upward. This posture is held as long as you can comfortably hold your breath, while imagining the *a* glowing hotter and hotter and making its vibration.

During the exhale, the electric hot tongue of fire flames up to melt the Thig-Le (the snow-white dot under the inverted seed-syllable HAM). This causes the bliss-creating nectar to drip into the rising liquid in the central channel. As this elixir reaches to the level of each chakra, it dissolves the obstructions there and flows out through the subtle energy pathways that radiate from it. Various kinds of bliss are thus experienced.[6]

By collecting and dissolving the vital airs of each chakra, death is simulated. At the time of death, the psychic knots at each chakra are relaxed and the vital airs spontaneously enter the central channel. This causes the appearance of the Clear Light of the Void. In meditation, we are able to remain focused on this and are not pulled into the karmic hallucinations of the second Bardo state. We can therefore attain a subtle body composed of vital airs and the mind of the meditational deity. This leads us to our eventual manifestation as a Buddha rather than incarnating again and again in a karmically formed existence in the phenomenal world.

The entire contents of the Mandala would then be held simultaneously in your awareness, and you would meditate on yourself as the Void in which it is all contained. The essential oneness that pervades that microcosm is your true nature. While reflecting, you would repeat these mantras:

OM SHUNYATA JNANA VAJRA SVABHAVA ATMAKOHAM

(I am the Void and Vajra Wisdom.)

---

[6]For more information on Vase Breathing and Heat Yoga, refer to *The Esoteric Teachings of Tibetan Tantra*, translated by Charles Muses from the original Chinese by Chang Chen Chi (York Beach, ME: Samuel Weiser, 1961), pp. 173–200.

OM VAJRA SHUDDHA SARVA DHARMA VAJRA SHUDDHOHAM

(I am pure Voidness which is the true nature of everything.)

To complete the meditation, imagine a white eight-petalled lotus in your third chakra. In the center of this lotus, seated on a moon disc, is Vajrasattva and his consort, Vajra Dignity. They are in the same posture that you meditated on them in the heart chakra in chapter 5. From the blue HUM in their hearts electric blue rays of light radiate in all directions throughout all the mandalas. Like the magnetic field of a magnet drawing iron filings, these blue rays attract all of the contents of your visualization and pull them back into you. Next your consort is absorbed into your body and you in turn shrink into Vajrasattva. As Vajrasattva, you absorb your consort into you and you shrink into the blue HUM in your heart. The HUM syllable then is absorbed into the small dot of light (*bindu*) over it. And finally the point of light fades into the Void like salt dissolving in water.[7]

As you proceed from meditation out into each day, you would imagine yourself to be Chakrasambhara or Vajra Yogini. When you eat, you are making offerings to yourself as a deity. When you go to the toilet, you are expelling obscurations from the world of sentient beings through your divine power. When you open a door, you are clearing the way to liberation for all beings. In this way you would think and act as if you were indeed the Devata at all times.

---

[7]This abridged version was paraphrased from the *Sri Chakra Sambhara Tantra*, edited by Kazi Dawa Sandup (London: Luzac & Co., and Calcutta: Thatcher, Spink & Co., 1919).

CHAPTER
EIGHT

◆

THE YONDER
SHORE

*T*he crown chakra is called *Sahasrara* in Sanskrit. It is the lotus of a thousand petals. The petals of this lotus hang downward to cover the Gate of Being—the anterior fontanel (the soft spot on a baby's head). This soft spot begins to harden around the age of six months, supposedly cutting off our connection to the spirit world. Ancient yogis developed practices to reopen it. It is said that if one can leave the body consciously through this Gate of Being at death, propelled by the last breath, liberation from the cycle of death and involuntary rebirth is attained.

On the petals of the lotus are the fifty letters of the Sanskrit alphabet (repeated twenty times, to make one thousand). These letters encircle the Sahasrara from right to left, and originate from the lines of the Supreme Triangle (Kamakala), the root of all sound in the center of this Supreme Lotus. The triangle symbolically forms the body of the primal unmanifested "sound" from which the universe is derived. The moon-like rays radiating from this luminous lotus are considered to be the nectar of immortality. See figure 34 on page 196.

The crown chakra in Buddhist Tantra is symbolized by a flaming blue drop of light (Thig-Le), which stands for the element of ether. The space-like quality of pristine consciousness, here in the top floor of the sacred temple, is presided over by Vairocana, the Primordial Buddha who represents the Wisdom of the Universal Law. His obscuring passions are delusion and ignorance. (See fig. 35 on page 198.)

From our psychological perspective, ideas pertaining to "God," the spiritual world, and our relationship to them are normally found lodged in this chakra. These concepts may originate from previous lifetimes, or from religious indoctrination in the

Figure 34. Sahasrara, the crown chakra, the thousand-petalled lotus, whiter than the full moon and tinged with the colors of the morning sun. Its rays are the nectar of immortality and on its petals are the fifty letters of the Sanskrit alphabet (repeated twenty times to make one thousand). In the center of this lotus is the supreme triangle, Kamakala, the primordial unmanifest "sound" of creation. Hindu texts vary considerably in their description of the complex symbolism related to this most sublime chakra. Its secrets are to be learned in meditation.

present life. They blind us to the intuitive awareness of the crown chakra. Often closely guarded by the ego, these sacred beliefs are quite difficult to question. Nonetheless, the importance of doing so cannot be overemphasized if we are to fathom the mystery and true nature of the Self.

The crown chakra also addresses our soul level of awareness. It is associated with mediumship and gives us access to the more sublime realms of the inner dimensions and to the spiritual beings that inhabit them.

The manifested form of the universe (including the various inner planes) is analogous to the body of the planet. Just as different species of animals and plants live in varying geographical and climatic conditions, a variety of "nonhuman" beings exist in other dimensions. The Deva kingdom, for example, includes an assembly of nature spirits who work in conjunction with the mineral and vegetable kingdoms. Perhaps the most well-known result of work with nature spirits today is the development of the incredible gardens at the Findhorn community in Scotland. In ancient cultures, rituals were actually used as a means of communicating and working with nature spirits.

Closely related to nature spirits are elementals, often associated with the forces of wind, water, fire and earth in various primitive and shamanic systems. Carlos Casteneda's books, for example, are full of accounts of his confrontations with these "allies" during his apprenticeship with Yaqui sorcerer Don Juan. Tibetan Tantra is no stranger to these elementals. For example, the Chöd ritual performed in chapter six was originally a way of communicating with and enlisting the aid of these strange disincarnate creatures who populate the lower realms of the astral plane.

Before we go on to discuss the beings who exist on the more spiritual levels of the inner planes, I want to clarify a small issue. Up to now in the text, I have presented the Buddhist viewpoint that all phenomena are illusory and dependent on subjective per-

Figure 35. Vairocana is the Dhyani Buddha who is lord of the crown chakra. He embodies the Dharmadhatu Wisdom. His color is blue and his element is Ether. He displays the Dharmachakra, or Teaching, Mudra. Plate 1 from *Foundations of Tibetan Mysticism*, by Lama Govinda (published in 1974 by Samuel Weiser, York Beach, Maine, and Rider & Co., London) reproduced here by permission of the publishers.

ception (which of course fits very comfortably with Jung's theory of the archetypes and how they are projected onto external experience). Later in this chapter I will qualify these positions. For now, let me say that these "non-physical" beings are no less real than we are. They, too, have a relative and temporally conditioned objective reality.

Each soul has at least one spiritual tutor, commonly referred to as a Spirit Guide. I find most people have several of these teachers and that we receive new teachers as we evolve. Although Spirit Guides may make suggestions to the soul, it is the soul's free choice and responsibility to follow the guidance offered. Because the ego-self is normally so divorced from our soul awareness, Spirit Guides are most influential in the period between lifetimes when we are given time to contemplate past lessons and make plans for the next life. The guides work very closely with us at these times.

From my experiences with past-life and in-between-life regressions, people who are primarily identified with the ego-self may not even realize that they are dead and may doze in dream-like hallucinations in the after-death state. For these people, the laws of karma work automatically and they are drawn into rebirth without much awareness of the process. Their guides appear as in dreams; any guidance given may or may not be acknowledged.

To the degree that we are awake on the soul level after death as well as during incarnation, we can learn from our guides. These guides may also be responsible for certain intuitive flashes and auspicious events in our lives. Regular periods of meditation and paying attention to dreams will increase receptivity to this inner guidance, which is very subtle, and often advises us in ways contrary to the wishes and demands of the ego.

In conclusion, the crown chakra level of consciousness is the central point from which the spider web of our individual identity originates. It is therefore the place where it is gathered back in, untangling the network of images which have composed our notion of self.

Beyond form, beyond thought, beyond concepts of being or non-being, consciousness plunges into the fathomless sea of the Clear Light of the Void through the Gate of Being in the crown chakra. As we integrate this peak experience we begin to identify with the whole-living-through-its-myriad-parts; the individual body-mind becomes a conscious hologram of the universe. There is nothing left to do but "Be," allowing the flow of creation to pass through unobstructed.

At this point the "soul complex" becomes immortal in the sense that it partakes of its Absolute Nature. Becoming a paradoxical individual expression of All-That-Is, we enter into a life of service and cooperation with cosmic forces and other beings who wield them.

◇

The Soul and
Its Journey

Our souls are like mere flickers of subatomic wave-particles in the cosmic matrix. Yet from our earthly perspective this flicker seems eternal. In fact, it is a common assumption that the soul is immortal, unchanging, and perfect. We have projected onto the concept of the soul some of the attributes of our most sublime body, the Bliss or Buddhic body. But even this body is not an entity or thing; it is a state of "Being-Consciousness-Bliss." As such it is inseparable from that which is eternal and unchanging. But the part of ourselves that is active in phenomenal realms, that part that survives death and transmigrates (the soul) is neither immortal nor unchanging. The Buddhists simply see it as a body of mental tendencies. It is born, evolves, and eventually goes through some "cosmic" type of death-rebirth experience.

Some souls begin their growing and learning long before coming to the earth. They come here for many reasons. In order to incarnate into the physical world the soul assumes the necessary bodies: the mental, emotional, etheric, and corporeal. These are its vehicles during its sojourn here. At death there is a gradual disintegration of these bodies as the soul draws back into itself.

The soul grows in awareness through the experiences of all its lifetimes. Not only do these accumulated adventures on the earth plane allow the soul to grow in understanding, they also play an important role in determining conditions of future lifetimes. If the seventh chakra is closed, the accumulated wisdom and purpose of the soul remains unconscious to the incarnate personality. On the other hand, an open seventh chakra becomes a channel of communication between the soul and the personality. Other lifetimes and a broad perspective on the various elements that define our individuality become apparent. When the soul's level of awareness begins to awaken in the body-mind, people from past lives are easily recognized, and we may more rapidly work through whatever karma we have with them.

The soul can be likened to the sun, and its various incarnations can be seen as planets. Each personality, from its space-time coordinate, views the other lifetimes as either ahead or behind it in their orbits. But the soul, at a certain level of development, may experience these many lifetimes, from its central or other-dimensional perspective, as occurring simultaneously. During the final stages of the soul's journey on the earth plane then, the balance of the psychic factors embracing all its lifetimes is brought more clearly into focus. They may be seen as a mandala in which the color and meaning of all the design factors interrelate to create the overall composition.

Souls are conditioned by their concepts of reality, but eventually they will need to relinquish their attachment to the dramas

and concepts that have composed their world views. Through
myriad incarnations, souls discover more and more of their innate
wisdom. After numerous experiments, and with the benevolent
tutorship of Spirit Guides, they gradually unfold their true
nature—Being-Consciousness-Bliss.

Though somewhat lengthy, I want to share the following
excerpt from a psychic reading because it is an excellent illustration of some of the trials that a soul goes through in search of its
spiritual nature.

I see that you are very pure and sincere in your desire to
develop spiritually. Previously, you have achieved higher
aspects of consciousness by being a hermit and directing
your attention fully inward. It is very hard for you to be
in physical form. You are very sensitive and find the
conditions of this world repulsive.

In order to be spiritual you feel you have to be separate
from the world. That is what is holding you back from
doing your teaching now. You need to understand that
you can be as spiritual in the world as you can be apart
from it.

Let's look at a couple of past lifetimes now, to give you a
better understanding of how these themes have developed. The first one I am seeing is a life as a Hindu holy
man. I'm getting two dates actually, one in the ninth
century and one in the 11th century. Apparently you
repeated the same pattern twice in a row.

Looking at your life in the ninth century, I see you as a
child in a family of ten children. Your parents are fairly
wealthy merchants. As you're growing up, you hear tales
and legends of holy men. You are enthralled and excited
by these stories of men who live in the mountains, riding

on tigers and doing other miraculous things. As a boy you often dream of someday being one of the holy men in the mountains . . . I see you now at the age of 20, working in your father's business and feeling trapped. The material world seems commonplace and you feel bored with it. You still hold this childhood image of the holy man and you carry with you the dream of transcendence and liberation. You don't know what this is all about, but it's something magical and burning inside you. I see you renouncing the family and becoming a wandering spiritual seeker. For the first several years this lifestyle is rather difficult for you because you are used to being well kept. You almost starve to death, and you become weary of traveling and walking. You go from ashram to ashram, experiencing different teachers. This process is very disillusioning because the fantasy you carry inside is not being fulfilled. You keep looking for that, and you're never satisfied.

I see that this search goes on for ten years. You have an intense desire to find out what transcendence is. Finally you go off into the mountains by yourself and become a hermit. During this period you reach a critical point of extreme disillusionment, yet there is nothing for you to turn back to. There is a real ego death in that—real surrender. I see another two or three years of living in the mountains this way. The only thing that fills your mind is to reach this state of consciousness which you feel is inherent within you. You collect wild plants and eat one small meal a day. You spend most of your time in meditation and filled with an ardent desire to reach liberation.

You are about 43 or 44 when you start having experiences of mystical states of consciousness. For the next ten years you continue to go deeper and deeper into this experience. I see you at the end of that time with a long white beard and hair. You never go back to civilization. You die up in the mountains. Although you reached high levels of consciousness, there is still part of you that isn't satisfied. Your preconceptions cause you to believe that you haven't reached the ultimate state. You leave this ninth century life with traces of dissatisfaction.

You reincarnate, still intent on your quest for liberation. This time you choose a poor family, so you don't get sidetracked by wealth or the comforts of life. I see you as a small boy leaving your family and going to a temple. You beg to be accepted into the monastic life. You are dismayed with the many rituals you have to perform. You remain in the temple, however, and advance spiritually rather quickly.

I see you now as a young man in the role of a high official of the temple. But still there is this burning knowingness inside—somehow this isn't what you are looking for. You feel guilty about misleading the people who come to the temple for religious guidance.

Around the age of 30 you once again become a wandering seeker, leaving the temple and renouncing your position. You find a teacher who lives in a small village in the mountains. You recognize him as an Enlightened Being. You feel very thankful, because you believe you've found what you've been looking for. I see you staying there for many years, eventually awakening Kundalini. During that time, you receive all you can from this teacher and you leave when you're about 45. As you leave, you have an image of going up into the Himalayas. This metaphor of going up into the mountains represents seeking the more rarified and purest states of consciousness. Once again you become a hermit. And yet there is still something more you're looking for. You have a picture, a concept, an underlying feeling that there is something more, a feeling that you are not understanding it all. So you die in this lifetime in the same attitude of seeking.

Because of your preconceptions about spirituality within the yogic tradition, you are deaf to help from your guides on the inner planes. Your soul is fixated on the concepts of liberation and Brahma (the Hindu concept of Absolute Reality). It is like a person growing up in the Christian tradition and expecting to be taken to heaven by a big man coming out of the clouds. You have died with the concept of reaching Nirvana and not having to return to Earth. You are so intent on this that it's a long time before you reincarnate again. You just won't listen to your guides. The mere thought of coming back to the Earth is repulsive to you. Finally, however, you are convinced that it is necessary to return and you are incarnated in the western world in an attempt to broaden your perspective on life—but, of course, you quickly make it to a monastery.

I see you as a Christian monk in Germany. You have a hard time relating your spiritual desires to the concepts of the Christian tradition. You transfer the concept of reaching Brahma to the Christian concept of God. This turns into an ardent desire and prayer to God to save you. In this life you are a cloistered monk; you live a completely alienated existence. You hardly ever relate to any of the other monks and refrain from any services that have to do with the public. You spend most of your time with yourself, meditating and copying scriptures. You're rather appalled by the level of intelligence of your fellow monks and their approach to God. On the other hand, you are at a loss to communicate your experiences to them. I see you meditating in the midst of incredible energies. The Kundalini energies that you had awakened in your previous life rise up within you again. But in the Christian tradition there are not many ways of understanding what is happening within you. You become attached to the Virgin Mary. You offer prayers to her as the Divine Mother and look to her for deliverance.

This time your soul is a little more agreeable after you die, and you receive quite a lecture from some of your guides about the benefits of working and serving humanity. They tell you that this is where you will find the deeper meaning that will satisfy and fulfill the longings that you are feeling. They convince you that it would be a good idea to try this approach.

I am seeing you as a small child, the first born of a family. This is just after the middle of the fifteenth century. Your father is a printer. You have a fairly normal, well-adjusted family life. I'm sensing a Bavarian atmosphere—there is a boisterous quality in your mother and father. As a young boy you spend quite a bit of time around the printed materials and you work in your father's print shop. The printed matter at that time is religious material, and you develop an ardent fever for reading. As you grow up you continue working with your father, but I also see you going to monasteries. You are interested in gathering more materials to be printed in order to spread the word of the scriptures.

In this life you get married. It is difficult for you to be intimate with another person. I'm seeing that your wife is very sensitive, meek, mild, and very dependent on you.

You feel the pressure of taking care of her. You also have a child, a male child. After several years, you take over your father's business. So there you are, the responsible business-family man. This weighs pretty heavily on you. It is a big pressure, and your ardent zeal in printing religious books and making them available to the public soon diminishes. You realize that your intention of inspiring the masses is not being realized. People still go on with their drinking and carrying on. So you become disillusioned. As time goes by, you have another child. You feel more and more trapped. There is no recourse for you – you are stuck with the business. You can't really make a living any other way and you feel obligated to the family. You live out the rest of this life feeling unhappy, and you die fairly young.

By this time your soul is immersed in disillusionment. Once again you're not available to advice from your guides and are sent immediately back into the world shrouded in your frustrations. You come into Italy during a time of much political unrest, a period in which there was a reformation in the Church and all the textbooks are being burned. I see you involved in that. You want to reform the world and purge everything. So this was an acting out of some of your frustration and disillusionment and the vehemence of your need to seek spiritual purity. You are totally consumed with this fanaticism. After you die in this life you are like a religious lunatic.

There is anger this time, a righteous anger. I am seeing you getting into some pretty severe confrontations with several of your guides. They really challenge you and break through the anger in an attempt to keep you in touch with the gentle essence of your spiritual nature.

The karma from that life is set aside for awhile and you
are guided to enter life in a female body. In this life you
are supposed to develop the feminine aspects of yourself, but you project your frustration and disillusionment
into your role as a woman. In this way you manage to
alienate yourself again.

Later in your present life, when you begin functioning as
a teacher, you will meet some of the same people that
you dealt with as a priest in the Counter-Reformation.
The nature of the karma is that you will need to learn
how to communicate, how to be with them in a way that
is going to help them, rather than alienate and condemn
them.

• • •

Whereas the body-mind is the vehicle, the soul is the driver.
Although dimly at first, the soul functions through the ego-self in
many lifetimes, growing in awareness of itself and the transpersonal dimensions of the cosmos. All of the archetypal themes
associated with the chakras are lived through by the soul. The
entire collection of these developmental patterns can be seen as
the labyrinth in which the soul eventually enters into the mysteries of its Being to receive its final initiation.

Up to now we have associated the seat of individual identity
with the ego-self. It should be apparent now that the fundamental
sense of separateness stems from the level of the soul. This "I" is
projected into the body-mind from the indwelling soul in various
incarnations. It is only during the soul's final hours that this "I"
becomes increasingly transparent.

◇

The Archetype
of the Self

In *Aion*, Jung identifies the Self as a "God-image." At least it cannot be distinguished from the God-image he qualifies. The polytheistic tendencies of ancient cultures demonstrate the richness of the archetypal levels of the psyche, but, as Jung goes on to point out, monotheism reveals the Self.[1]

The image of God, projected from the spiritual depths of the soul, was also called the transcendent function by him because its power can move us beyond the dualism of our "I-ness." Transforming symbols emerge from the Self that inspire us to seek out our wholeness. Like a river, we are driven to return to our source. It's as if life itself is evolving through us, plunging ever onward to merge into the Boundless Ocean of Being-Consciousness. The end of our journey is near. What is the nature of the transformation that lies just ahead? In order to put the answer to this question into perspective, let's sum up Jung's process of individuation by referring to the religious symbolism of our native culture and the Christ symbol. Again in *Aion*, Jung speaks of Christ as our cultural hero, and regardless of his historical reality, it is he who abides at the center of the Christian mandala as the exemplar of the Self.[2]

Jesus was reportedly born in the aura of auspicious divine signs, and his name means "Messiah," or savior, in Hebrew. According to the Hebrew scriptures, it was prophesied that a savior would be born, in the family lineage of David, to be King of

---

[1]Carl Jung, *Aion*, Bollingen Series, Vol. IX (Princeton, NJ: Princeton University Press, 1959), p. 22.
[2]Jung, *Aion*, pp. 36–37.

the Jews. The Hebrews had suffered oppression, conflict, and exile throughout their history, which can be traced back to ancient Ur and Chaldea, about 2000 B.C. Their scriptures speak of suffrage in the context of their attempts and failures to comply with the sometimes wrathful and sometimes benevolent God, Yahweh. The prophets of the Old Testament looked forward to the coming of a leader who would lead them back into righteousness and peace. Jesus was hailed as this spiritual King by a relatively small number of Jews.

It is said that upon baptism by John, Jesus was overshadowed by the "Holy Ghost" and the "Spirit of God" entered him. He thus became known as the Christ (a Greek word that means, "the Lord's anointed one," or "king by divine right") by those who believed Jesus to be the awaited Messiah.

Looking at the context of Jesus' life and the nature of his impact, we can see a perfect metaphor of the trials and tribulations of ego-consciousness and the redeeming action of the Self. In the midst of the political turmoil of Roman oppression, conflicting religious divisions, Messianic hopes, and revolutionary feverment, Jesus "the Christ" appears as the messenger of the peace and wholeness within. (Another name associated with Christ is Emmanuel, "God within"). The image of Christ is, therefore, the archetype of the transpersonal and whole-making aspects of the psyche. In psychological terms, then, Christ is the mediator, or exemplar, of the Self in relationship to the ego.

The symbolism of the crucifixion, for instance, dramatically illustrates the psychology of ego-death and the necessity of reconciling the opposition within the psyche. The transpersonal reality of the Self can no longer be escaped and the personal identity is hung on the cross, which represents the quaternity of opposites integrated in their central or transcendent convergence.

Until we reach this critical level of unfoldment, the underlying tension and dualism of the psyche is not so apparent. During the previous stages of ego development, we have identified with the ego, which organizes the awareness of psychic contents into logical categories while repressing those elements that threaten its integrity. We were, therefore, clinging desperately to one side of the polarity while avoiding the other. Jung goes on to point out that whenever there is an accentuation of the Christ image it stimulates a simultaneous activation of the shadow, its unconscious complement, and hence the tension between the two is increased.[3]

It is through love and acceptance of all parts of ourselves that our psychological redemption occurs. And this is precisely what the Christ-image, as an expression of the Self, requires of us. In the Christian myth, Christ is considered to be the Son of God; that is, the incarnation of God, who is sometimes equated with pure love. Psychologically, this represents the all-inclusiveness of the Self.

The transpersonal qualities of the Self seek to be realized within the personal boundaries of the ego-consciousness, just as the ego-bound consciousness is driven eventually to enter the domain of the transpersonal. The legendary figure of Jesus Christ is actually a model for the type of being anyone can become when thus transfigured. The resurrection and ascension are mythogems connoting transcendence of the temporal and personal conditions of ego-centered existence.

Whether we speak of a Buddha or a Christed being, there is a radical transformation that occurs when we surrender to the Self. It seems that Jung approached these portals, but because the possibility of enlightenment does not appear in his accounts of the individuation process, we might conclude that he did not pass through. He maintains that the goal of individuation is never fully realized, it is only a process that leads *toward* wholeness. In other

---

[3]Jung, *Aion*, p. 43.

words, it is not an end, but the means through which the process
of transpersonal integration occurs.

Ultimately, the ego was viewed by Jung as a vessel that
continues to grow to eventually circumscribe and contain an endless fount of symbolic expressions of the Self. This Self, however,
remains transcendent—a hidden and unreachable goal, according
to Jungian analyst Aniela Jaffe in *The Myth of Meaning*.[4]

Jung undoubtedly touches on a great mystery here, but even
though all the potential of the Self can never be assimilated by the
rational self, superior levels of consciousness unfold in which the
Great Mystery is fathomed. The rapture of a mystic is a very real
event profoundly affecting the personal self. In her autobiogra-
phy, *The Life of Teresa of Jesus*, St. Teresa speaks of visions and
raptures that have a wonderfully purifying effect. Elaborating, she
says that these effects are like a great flame which consumes our
sensual natures and all of life's desires. What remains is a profound reverence.[5]

Extraordinary spiritual phenomena, like those commonly
associated with holy men in the East, were attributed to St.
Teresa. For example, she was prone to levitation, and when she
died her body smelled like fresh flowers and did not decompose!
Similarly, St. Catherine of Siena experienced ecstatic raptures
during which her body rose into the air and emitted a sweet
fragrance. In these trance states, she sometimes verbalized an
outpouring of "God-intoxicated" dialogues. She later composed
some of these, recorded by observers, into the *Divine Dialogues*.
In these dialogues she speaks of seeing the hidden things of God
that cause her to burst with supreme splendor and to be transformed in "His" immeasurable providence. She says that though
the soul is satiated by these experiences it still remains hungry to

---

[4]Aniela Jaffe, *The Myth of Meaning* (New York: Penguin, 1971), p. 120.
[5]*The Life of Teresa of Jesus*, quoted in *The Laughing Man*, Vol. 2, No. 2, Dawn
Horse Press, 1981, p. 50.

see God in His light and by His light. It is this light that has shown her His truth and the highest and infinite Good–Beauty beyond all Beauty, and Wisdom beyond all Wisdom.

Another example was the mystic Jan Van Ruysbroeck, who retreated into the forest when the Holy Spirit moved him. Once, after a prolonged absence, several monks went to find him. They discovered him seated under a tree which was aflame with light. He was lost in ecstasy and surrounded by a brilliant aura of Divine Light.

Ruysbroeck was a Flemish contemporary of Meister Eckhart. He was a prolific author of mystical literature, nearly escaping the censorship of the Church, and thus not sharing Eckhart's fate as a heretic. Echoing Eckhart, Ruysbroeck wrote in *The Sparkling Stone*, that those who see God intuitively transcend all distinctions and are transfigured by an inborn light with which they are united and through which they see.[6]

Could this inborn light, or the luminous Holy Spirit of God's grace, reported by these Christian mystics actually be the Clear Light of the Void? When we read the accounts of mystics from various spiritual traditions, the most common reference to God we find is that of a supernal light. Is it necessary, or even helpful, to superimpose an image of God on this experience of the Absolute? In *The Blissful Life*, Robert Powell tells the life story of a modern Hindu holy man, Shri Nisargadatta Maharaj, who says he has never seen God and knows nothing of normal religious things. Seeing the world like the illusion created on a movie screen, he knows that it is the light (pure awareness) which illuminates the projection of the ever-changing images. He entertains no idea of an external God because he has realized that "I am That" (the light of pure awareness).[7]

---

[6]The above mentioned material was discussed in an article from *The Laughing Man*, Vol. 2, No. 2, Dawn Horse Press, 1981, pp. 46, 61–62.
[7]Robert Powell, *The Blissful Life* (Durham, NC: Acorn Press, 1984), p. 27.

$$\diamond$$

Essence of the
Wisdom Gone
Beyond

The theory of Voidness was expounded in various ways in the development of Buddhism. The following Heart Sutra, supposedly preached by Buddha (500 B.C.), is an example of the non-rational, or devotional, approach.

> Thus I have heard: Once the Blessed One was dwelling in Rajagriha on Vulture's Peak together with a great assembly of monks and Bodhisattvas. At that time the Blessed One was totally absorbed in the concentration that examines all phenomena, called "Profound Illumination."

> At the same time the Noble Avalokitesvara . . . was looking at the profound practice of the Wisdom Gone Beyond, analyzing the five aggregates, by nature empty.

> Then, through the inspiration of Buddha, the venerable Shariputra spoke to the Noble Avalokitesvara . . . saying, "How should those of good family learn who wish to follow the profound practice of the Wisdom Gone Beyond?"

> Thus he spoke and the Noble Avalokitesvara . . . replied to the venerable Shariputra: "O Shariputra, whatever son or daughter of a good family wishes to follow the profound practice of the Wisdom Gone Beyond should look at it like this, analyzing the five aggregates, by nature empty.

"Form is empty, emptiness is form. Emptiness is no other than form, form is no other than emptiness. In the same way, feeling, recognition, karmic formations and consciousness are all empty. Therefore, Shariputra, all phenomena are empty, without characteristics. They are unborn and unceasing; they are neither impure nor free from impurity. They neither decrease nor increase.

"Therefore, Shariputra, in emptiness there is no form, no feeling, no recognition, no karmic formations, no consciousness; there is no eye, no ear, no nose, no tongue, no body, no mind. . . . There is no ignorance nor is there destruction of ignorance. There are none of these all the way up to there is no old age and death nor is there destruction of old age and death. Thus there is no suffering, no cause of suffering, no cessation of suffering and no path. There is no wisdom, no attainment and no non-attainment.

"Therefore, Shariputra, because there is no attainment, all Bodhisattvas hold to the Wisdom Gone Beyond and because there is no obscurity of mind they have no fear. Passing utterly beyond falsity, they reach beyond the bounds of sorrow. All the Buddhas who dwell in the three times, by relying on the Wisdom Gone Beyond fully and clearly awaken to the unsurpassed, most perfect and complete Enlightenment . . .

"O Shariputra, this is how a Bodhisattva Mahasattva should learn the profound Wisdom Gone Beyond."

Then the Blessed One arose from that concentration and praised the Noble Avalokitesvara . . . saying, "Very good, very good, O son of good family. It is exactly like that. The profound Wisdom Gone Beyond should be

practiced exactly as you have said and Those Who Have
Thus Gone will rejoice . . ."[8]

In *Tibetan Yoga and Secret Doctrines*, W. Y. Evans-Wentz suggests that the Doctrine of Voidness was a revamping of the Hindu
teachings of Maya (the Great Illusion) by the great Buddhist
philosophers who inspired the Mahayana form of Buddhism. He
also mentions that it is generally believed that Buddha esoterically
taught the Prajna-Paramita (Wisdom Gone Beyond) about six
hundred years earlier to his most advanced students.[9] Nonetheless the teachings on Voidness were not presented exoterically
until the second century A.D.

The Buddhist philosopher Nagarjuna reportedly received the
teachings in a heaven realm, where Gautama Buddha had supposedly hidden them, and articulated a negative dialectic (the
Madhyamika philosophy) to logically prove the theory of Voidness. Later the Mahasiddha Yogis (approximately 700–1000
A.D., at the height of Indian Tantric Buddhism) existentially
reacted to the analytical methods of the Mahayana Sutras to
practice experiential Tantric methods. The philosophical logic of
the Sutras and the experiential techniques of the Tantras were
thus combined into a body of teachings known as Mahamudra.

In advanced levels of meditation, the Clear Light of the Void
generates an extremely blissful state of awareness. This ecstasy
transcends every other pleasure, and is therefore "great" (maha).
Once we have experienced the Bliss and Plenum of the Void, we
can never forget it, the experience is sealed (mudra) in our minds,
which explains the meaning of the Great Seal or Mahamudra.

The First Pachem Lama, in *The Great Seal of Voidness*, gives a
hidden etymology for the Tibetan term for Mahamudra, Chaggya
Chenpo. "Chag" refers to Voidness, "gya" is liberation from sam-

---

[8]The Heart Sutra.
[9]W. Y. Evans-Wentz, *Tibetan Yoga and Secret Doctrines* (Oxford: Oxford University Press, 1958), pp. 344, 349.

sara and "Chenpo" signifies the great unification of the realization of Voidness and the liberation from the world view of illusion (samsara). He also offers another meaning for Mahamudra. "Mudra" means necessary prerequisite. "Maha" means great understanding. Hence there is no technique for attaining Enlightenment without a profound understanding of Voidness.[10]

The methods of the Sutras begin with a philosophical analysis of Voidness and proceed to meditation techniques for quieting the mind. Once controlled and focused, the mind is used in meditation to prove the philosophical understanding of voidness through penetrative insight into the nature of mind itself. Tantric methods emphasize the purification of the psychic forces in the chakras that sustain the functions of the ego-mind, and their articulation into the central energy channel along the spine. When the mind is cleansed of its phenomenal obscurations, the Clear Light of the true nature of the mind shines forth spontaneously.

In order to attain the Great Seal, Mahamudra, the mind must be prepared. The most difficult and important part of growing a garden, for instance, is the initial preparation of the soil. Likewise, the mind must be made ready to receive the seeds of wisdom that the Mahamudra teachings offer. If it is not properly trained it may mistake ideas about the Void for the experience itself, or entertain nihilistic misconceptions. To begin let's gain insight into how the mind creates the "wrong view" of the world.

The Buddhists maintain that our ordinary perception of the world is a collective hallucination developed since the beginning of the history of consciousness. This collective illusion was created by a mental process called "labeling" in which the rational mind perceives a group of convergent factors and selectively organizes them into an object. A name, or label, is then assigned to the object and it assumes the status of "reality." The mind actually

---

[10] The First Pachem Lama, *The Great Seal of Voidness* (Dharamsala, India: Library of Tibetan Works and Archives, 1975), p. 7.

creates its own reality through interpreting the constant flux of forces and substances as they appear to assume particular forms in isolated segments of space and time. This reality is nothing more than a collection of images or concepts in the mind.

The Buddhists illustrate how we are born into this hallucination with the metaphor of a tent lit up from the inside by the glow of a hundred butter lamps. Standing outside the tent we do not notice if one of these lamps expires or another is lit. In the same way, the collective illusion of the world continues, imperceptibly affected by individual deaths and rebirths.

The major focus of the penetrative insight of Tantric Buddhism is to undermine the "ordinary view." This is a very tedious and difficult task. Not only has the mind been indoctrinated by this view, it has an innate propensity to create this deluded viewpoint.

The lack of "inherent existence" is also an important concept in comprehending the meaning of voidness. To exist inherently means to be independent of any conditioning factor. But nothing in the phenomenal world exists independent of the parts that compose it and the label that the mind has placed on the appearance of the composite of transient elements. But our normal view of reality is founded entirely on the illusion of people and things possessing inherent or independent existence. For example a car does not have inherent existence. When we remove all of the mechanical parts that together compose it, there is no car remaining. "Car" is just a label, a concept in the mind projected onto the appearance of a unique assembly of components.

The entire fortress of ego-consciousness is built on the ordinary view of external reality and a similarly attained belief in an independent and concrete sense of self. Our sense of "I" is an unquestioned a priori assumption. However, it is merely a label— it does not exist inherently. When we search for this "I" in meditation, it is nowhere to be found.

Another important aspect of gaining a "right view" is the understanding that the "things" that are labeled in our conventional concepts of reality do possess certain qualities. These qualities can be experienced in their rawness when we clear away our preconceptions of what an object is. Empirical phenomena do have a relative objective existence which does not contradict their essential voidness. It is indeed the voidness of things (lack of inherent existence) that allows the phenomenal world to unfold and change; its protean qualities would be destroyed if its elements possessed independent existence and remained fixed in their natures.

The Void is therefore contingent with the appearance of the phenomenal world. Appearance in the mind (of the reality of objects) is inseparable from the void nature of pristine consciousness in the same way that the reflection of the moon on the water is inseparable from the mirroring surface of the water. Furthermore, we cannot actually measure and define the Void, words like essence or spirit are as close as we can come, but they still imply "some-thing." Edwin Bernbaum, in *The Way to Shambhala*, offers this metaphor: it as a clear and indestructible emptiness—like a sparkling diamond—that we find at the core of ourselves and pervading all things. He goes on to say that when we experience this reality things do not disappear, they become translucent, like wax paper lanterns which are illuminated by the Clear Light of the Void.[11]

Nihilism can be called a repudiation of the authenticity of experiences, and therefore a denial of any associated meaning or value. The negative implications of nihilism lead to hopelessness and futility. While the theory of Voidness suggests that searching for meaning in the phenomenal world is for the most part an egoistic attempt to validate our existence, it does not encourage a

---

[11]Edwin Bernbaum, *The Way to Shambhala* (New York: Doubleday, Anchor, 1980), pp. 108–109.

pessimistic view of existence. Chogyam Trungpa, in *Cutting Through Spiritual Materials*, says that instead of looking for some great profundity in events and things, we need to understand that things are just what they are.[12]

He goes on to share the story of how some of the arhats (literally "victorious ones," *i.e.*, Buddha's advanced students) died of heart attacks when Buddha gave his first teachings on Voidness.[13] These students had apparently experienced melting into space in meditation, but they were still relating to space as "something." They were still involved in a dualistic experience of subject and object. The impact of the theory of Voidness, which involves being "nowhere" and experiencing "no-thing," was devastating to their sense of reality.

Nagarjuna further developed the implications of the theory of Voidness by propounding that we cannot even begin to consider the nature of reality. To do so would require a dualistic approach—an observer separate from reality who can perceive, define, and name it. The concept of "tathata" (suchness) thus became associated with the theory of Voidness. The phenomenal world just is. The process by which it arises and fades away just is. The emptiness of space and the emptiness of the mirror-like quality of pristine consciousness just is.

Even if we agree that reality is a mystery, we are affirming that it is "some-thing." Trungpa points out that belief in any philosophy or religion, from the viewpoint of Nagarjuna's Madhyamika teachings, is merely a process of projecting a label on the mystery. Furthermore, he continues, since there is no one to perceive reality, and no concepts resulting from this perception;

---

[12]Chogyam Trungpa, *Cutting Through Spiritual Materialism* (Boston: Shambhala, 1973), p. 189.

[13] Trungpa, *Cutting Through Spiritual Materialism*, p. 190.

things and events arise in the sky-like openness of lucid awareness in their suchness.[14]

In a more modern context, the implications of the Theory of
Voidness are demonstrated in Einstein's Unified Field Theory.
The findings of contemporary physics further emphasize that a
separate, self-contained existence is an impossibility. There are
no hard boundaries in the great matrix of multi-dimensional energies that the universe is. When we relinquish our insistence on
the illusionary boundaries created by the rational mind, the infinite energy of "all that is" meets with no impedance as it moves
through the body-mind. Liberated from the mental constructs of
the serial structure of time and space, we experience mass,
energy, and consciousness as a unified field.

The Clear Light of the Void does not change and is not
dependant on any cause. Like a mirror, it remains unaffected by
whatever appearances are reflected in it. The maintenance of the
clarity of the Void in our everyday experiences is symbolized by
the fish in Buddhist Tantra. In the *Masters of Mahamudra*, Keith
Dowman describes how the fish swims effortlessly, unblinking
and apparently never sleeping, through its environment. In addition, fish don't get wet; they are in the water but not of it.[15] For
the ancient yogis, the fish was a metaphor for how we can be in
the phenomenal world once we become buddhas.

Dowman goes on to illustrate one of the last obstacles on the
path in the biography of the Mahasiddha Kanhapa—the meditator
who realizes the Clear Light of the Void in meditation, but whose
realization is lost once engaged in the dramas of day to day
existence.[16] The practice of Mahamudra therefore ultimately
involves a transference of the experience of Voidness into daily

---

[14] Trungpa, *Cutting Through Spiritual Materialism*, p. 194, 196.
[15] Keith Dowman, *Masters of Mahamudra* (Albany, NY: State University of New
York Press, 1985), p. 78.
[16] Dowman, *Masters of Mahamudra*, pp. 123–129.

activities. Life itself is the path. Every obstacle, problem, or desire is an opportunity to release ego grasping and acknowledge the inseparableness of appearances and the Void. By itself, without effort, life will present the very experiences and situations that reveal where we need to let go of discursive thoughts, aversions, and desires. No matter the event, feeling or conceptual orientation, all is an opportunity to practice Mahamudra. Relinquishing all desires and conceptual fabrications related to actions from the past, present, and future, and developing an uninterrupted state of meditational equipoise throughout the fantastic dream of life, we eventually integrate the primordial state of Being-Consciousness-Bliss into our day to day existence.

Through the course of understanding the flux of consciousness through the chakras, we have gained some awareness of our instinctual predispositions, the occurrence of feelings and emotions, and the tendencies in our minds. We are now at a point where we can experience the emptiness of these phenomena— there is no self inherent in these events. Once the illusion of self identity is dispelled, our experience in the world is radically altered. No longer enslaved by the ego, we assume a non-self-directed and spontaneous mode of action. Life becomes awesomely simple, there is only one response to whatever life brings our way—unconditional acceptance and compassion.

$$\diamondsuit$$

The Gift of the Dakini

Not long after I was introduced to Tibetan Buddhism, I had the following experiences. At that time my knowledge of the various deities and more advanced practices was very limited. I was not under the personal guidance of any teacher during this time, although I had taken refuge with Karmapa and received some lesser teachings and initiations. The events that follow took place entirely spontaneously. (I might add that this was not my first experience with Kundalini. About ten years earlier I had been inspired to live in the woods like a yogi on retreat. During that time I had my initial experience with the awakening of Kundalini.) Several years after the events that I am about to share took place, I attended a Mahamudra retreat and was initiated into higher Tantric practices. Although I have had the experiences recorded below, and have had the Mahamudra initiations and instructions, I do not feel that I can write about these final stages of the Tantric path with any genuine authority, nor, if I could, do I think it would be ultimately of great value to you. I therefore choose to conclude with the diary of my relationship to the dakini who introduced me to the realization symbolized in higher Tantric practices in hopes of inspiring you to seek out the only viable source of knowledge – your own experience.

While the Tantric tradition emphasizes a relationship to an incarnate guru, Tantric lore also contains many legends of yogis who received initiations from dakinis who appeared to them in dreams, meditation, or in the form of an incarnate woman. Modern research also indicates that Kundalini can awaken spontaneously outside of a student-teacher relationship – in most cases, I assume, due to previous lifetimes in which it had been developed. Or in other situations, the archetypal forces at play may be surfacing of their own accord.

In sharing this excerpt from my meditation diary, I hope to convey the intrinsic value of the symbols and experiences as they appeared naturally. By so doing I hope to impress upon the reader that these deities, i.e., their qualities of consciousness, do indeed exist in the more sublime dimensions of the psyche.

Figure 36. Vajra Vahari Mandala. In this meditation mandala, Vajra
Vahari is surrounded by four dakinis. Each stands in a dance posture
and appears to be identical with Vajra Vahari except for their color and
the ornaments on their vajra knives, which identifies each with one of
the five Buddha families. Vajra Vahari emanates from the cosmic
womb, symbolized by an inverted triangle. Her color is red and she is
radiant with bliss; the primordial energy associated with the inner fire
(Dumo). From the Thanka collection of Sergei Diakoff, used by
permission.

March 8, 1980

A female spirit came to me today while I was meditating. She asked me to meditate regularly and to refrain from sexual encounters for several months; in turn she would aid me in my spiritual practice. To my surprise she then sat astride me in the Tantric yabyum position. I felt an intense exchange of psychic energy, especially in the left and right channels along the spine (Ida and Pingala). This profound experience of the resonance between us inspired me to reflect on the ancient sexual practices of Tantra. This led to a spontaneous recall of a life as a woman Tantric teacher in ancient India. After this meditation experience, I was very intrigued and was left in a state of expectancy.

March 9

The dakini began the meditation today by drawing a circle around me on the floor. Within the circle she drew a six-pointed star (two interlocking triangles). She then assumed the yabyum position and I began to feel a powerful sense of grounding. I also became aware of a concentration of energy in my first chakra and then noticed that my "consort" was sucking energy from her left and right channels into her first chakra. This was creating a vacuum in my own energy system which was drawing energy into my first chakra.

Again I was amazed by the resonance between us. It felt like two voices singing in harmony: the merging of the two energies created something that is more than the sum of its two parts. I felt a tremendous peace and an overall balancing of my energy field. (The mandala of the two interlocking triangles was the only clue that I had to assigning an identity to the dakini who was instructing me. It is the mandala of the goddess Vajra Vahari, the goddess associated with the Dumo fire in Tibetan Tantra. See figure 36 on page 224.)

March 10

Today my guide sat in front of me and my attention was again drawn to the first chakra. I noticed that the left and right channels that meet there were larger today. Then the place where they meet seemed to open up and the channels turned upward like two snakes to enter the central channel. After about fifteen minutes I felt a dense energy begin to move up the central channel. The image of a glass tube being filled with a golden liquid came to mind. When the golden liquid got to the level of my third chakra it was blocked from moving higher by a dark thick substance in the tube. After the pressure built up for awhile, the denser energy was pushed upward and I felt it running up through my chest and out my arms. Continuing to rise, the golden liquid spewed out the top of my head. I became a fountain of golden light.

My guide then came and sat in the yabyum position. This caused the flow of energy in the central channel to increase. I felt a great deal of warmth and love as we sat embracing in this shower of golden energy. I also had an uncanny feeling of being opened up from the inside out. Layer after layer seemed to peel away, revealing vast horizons of inner space. Eventually, everything was stripped away and there was nothing left, no me, no guide, no-thing except a lucid golden light. I have no idea how long I remained in this state. Returning, I felt like a Buddha radiating light out in all directions.

March 11

Meditation began today once again with the drawing of the circle and interlocking triangles. As my guide assumed the yabyum position, she told me to visualize myself as Vajrasattva. As I did this, I had a vivid flashback to an initiation that I received from Gongpo Tsedam Rinpoche, and I experienced the same expansiveness that I had at that time. This expanding continued until my body was the entire cosmos. There were spirals within spirals of energy within me. Planets spiraled around the sun as it spiraled around the galactic center, which itself moved through the space of my cosmic body. There were two main spirals of energy moving up and down the length of my spine. These were so powerful that my whole body was gyrating.

I then felt a unification of the forces that flowed back and forth from the crown to the first chakra. This resulted in a concentration of forces in the heart chakra—it felt like a million suns radiating waves of compassion and love. This was amplified by the tremendous power I was feeling in the union with my consort. I felt that we were the heart of creation and that all the polarities of life emanated from us.

I had a profound sense that everything was contained within me. My guide told me that the Vajrasattva yabyum was all encompassing, that it is the state prior to entering the Void. She then brought me into the Void. The intense movement of energies within me became static, and a brilliant white light burst into my awareness. I felt like I was going to explode and there was an excruciating pressure in my sixth chakra. This lasted only a short while. Afterward, I felt a deep peace while a high-pitched ringing echoed through my higher chakras. A warmth welled up within me and I began to cry. Powerful feelings of love were surfacing from deep within me—the feelings that I have sought in relationships. I was overwhelmed with gratitude as I realized that this love is "mine," or actually, I am it! This love can never be taken away.

March 12

Today my guide began by drawing the encircled six-pointed star beneath me. I felt that my aura was being sealed and grounded within this mandala as she sat in front of me. I began feeling a sensation in my etheric body. It started in my pelvis and moved up through my stomach and chest. The front of my torso felt like it was being stretched and opened. This sensation moved up and over my head, then down through my neck, shoulders, and upper spine. As it moved down through the lumbar region I felt some blockages there being opened. The force then moved down into my legs to open the constricted energy at the knees. After the force circulated down through my feet and back up to the pelvis, my etheric body began pulsating with light.

My guide came to sit in the yabyum position. I noticed that the right and left channels seemed even larger today. While focusing on this, I realized that my guide had actually merged her subtle energy system with mine. As the flow of Kundalini rose up the central channel, it seemed much more powerful today, and I moved very quickly into the Void. The pressure in my higher chakras was more intense and the light appeared to be more blinding.

At the end of the meditation, all of this intensity was concentrated in my throat chakra. My guide telepathically told me that my throat center was being programmed to develop new neurological circuits in my nervous system.

March 13

This morning my guide began by standing in front of me and draining some dark energy out of my astral body. I could see a whirlpool of astral energy at the level of the second chakra, about two feet in front of me. She pulled the funnel of this whirlpool out to the edge of my aura where it dissipated. My guide continued to stand in front of me and I could feel something happening in my astral body. She told me that she was placing an image of Vajrasattva in my aura; by visualizing me as this Buddha she was purifying my astral body. She then told me to assume the identity of Vajradhara and as I did, the vibration in my aura intensified. I felt tremendous joy and a profound sense of peace. I felt confident and triumphant—exalted. I felt the pressure in my upper chakras again, this became so strong that it became increasingly difficult to breathe (my breath actually seemed to stop several times). At the end of the session today, the energy was so thick, yet clear, that I felt my body had turned into crystal glass.

March 14

For about an hour and a half my guide and I sat in the yabyum position while focusing on the first chakra. I had trouble with remaining concentrated on the intensification of the Kundalini there. By the end of the session however, I was virtually ringing with energy.

The dakini telepathically informed me that my lifetimes in the Tibetan tradition created a vehicle of consciousness that was more perfected than in any other lives, and that I was reuniting with it now. This caused me to recall my first psychic reading. The psychic had told me that I reached enlightenment in a past life as a Tibetan lama. This confused me at the time; I couldn't imagine being enlightened in a past life and being such a mess in this one. I had a preconception that when you reach enlightenment, that's it, you never have to come back. I understand more clearly now that in each life we retrace a lot of our footsteps on the spiritual path. Even though we may have a breakthrough in one life, we still have many karmic patterns that need to be played out in order to be exhausted. We may have later lives in which our developed levels of realization are not fully expressed as these patterns play themselves out and our inner knowingness is tempered. Life isn't always lived high in the Himalayas! There's also the probability of subsequently misusing the power and knowledge for self-aggrandizement, which creates more and very potent karma.

March 16

As my guide assumed the yabyum position at the beginning of the session, she once again intensified the flow of energy in the right and left channels into the central channel. After about an hour, a cleansing force traveled back up the right and left channels to meet in the sixth chakra. This caused a brilliant golden light to radiate from the sixth chakra. This light then moved down through the right and left channels, increasing the force through them and into the central channel.

For the rest of the session, I experienced new levels of energy rushing up the central channel. I was rapt, in an ecstatic bliss embracing my consort. These dimensions of awareness have been inside me all along; it is this state that I have longed for. It is like a dream come true to return to this tranquil bliss. I am filled with gratitude to receive this grace.

March 17

Today the session started as usual, with my guide assuming the yabyum position. For about fifteen minutes she created a vacuum in her central channel to stimulate the energy in my central channel. Soon there was a river of white-golden light flowing from my first to seventh chakra. This river of light kept increasing in volume and velocity. Suddenly the river became static, and level after level of light dimensions dawned from within the core of the central channel. I occasionally slipped into hypnagogic states and saw visions, but was able to pull myself back to keep the clarity of the Void. I feel stunned now, my ears are ringing and there is a high vibration buzzing throughout my body.

March 18

Today's session was virtually the same as yesterday, except that prior to entering the Void my guide brought in the image of Manjusri. He carries a sword in his right hand that symbolizes the clarity that cuts through the illusion of samsara. In his left hand he holds the Dharma, a book that contains the wisdom of the higher states of consciousness realized in meditation. My guide instructed me to contemplate the veneer quality of ordinary reality. I was then once again immersed into the infinite ocean of light and peace.

I am left with an insight: the freedom gained from cutting the attachment of the ego is synonymous with prosperity! "When we lose ourselves we gain the Source of all."

March 19

As the golden river of light flowed up the central channel today, my head spontaneously fell forward; my chin pressed against my chest. This dammed the flow of the river, which became still and silent. After a while, my head lifted and I entered the Void. A translucent image of a primordial Buddha (I later identified him as the Dhyani Buddha Vairocana) appeared, and I identified with his meditational awareness. This caused me to experience a profound solemnness; a stillness much deeper than the words peace and tranquility can convey. I was at the bottom of an ocean of stillness; the manifested world was so far above that its surface was totally "out of mind and sight."

March 20

Things began as usual this morning, but soon took an interesting course. My consort seemed to be deliberately arousing sexual feelings in me. I was shocked, but have been learning to trust these experiences. I actually got an erection as her beautiful etheric form danced erotically before me. Powerful sexual feelings overwhelmed me as she came to unite with me in the yabyum posture. I suddenly had a strong reaction, I felt uncomfortable with the intensity of the sexual feelings—"I'd rather be meditating in the Void! " (a good bumper sticker). At this realization, the sexual energy subsided. I understood that my guide was encouraging me to make an important decision. If the power that I am being initiated into was allowed to feed old sexual-romantic patterns, I would be enslaved by them. I was shown how this, in fact, had happened in a past life, and how these attachments have affected me in this life. I understood this, but there was still a part of me pleading: "Isn't there a woman with whom I could enjoy Tantric sexuality?"

A very interesting thing happened after I agreed to release my attachments. My first chakra seemed to be a vagina and there was a large penis rising up within it. It grew in size until it ascended to my crown chakra. This was accompanied with strong physical sensations and a powerful sense of the strength of the lingam. The lingam-yoni metaphor evoked a potent sense of fulfillment and self-containment. After about ten minutes of enjoying this state, the lingam began to expand out into infinity. Once again I was dissolved into the Void.

March 21

In today's session, my guide concentrated on my mental body. I had images of my mind being like a computer chip that was being plugged into the cosmic mind-computer. As this took place, a very high frequency vibration and a resplendent light moved from the top of my mental body down into the crown chakra. These focused in the sixth chakra, and my head felt like it was going to burst. As my awareness diffused out into the universal mind, it entered an infinite sea of light-consciousness. From this perspective, I saw endless waves of life rolling out toward the shores of the phenomenal worlds. I saw innumerable worlds being created and destroyed by these waves. The essential meaninglessness of these cosmic pulses inspired a great joy and sense of release in me. I don't really know why.

March 22

Today my mental body felt very large and heavy—like a big brass bell. On top of it, I had a vision of my soul sitting in the form of Vajradhara. This Buddha seemed to emanate from the heart of space—the deepest Self. I felt boundless and serene as my awareness was drawn back into this level.

March 23

My guide began by asking me to review what I had experienced yesterday. As I did, a large amount of psychic energy poured down through the crown chakra into my sixth and fifth chakras. I thought that I was being empowered to manifest these levels of consciousness in my life. When these forces moved down into my heart center, I was overcome with peace and a distinct sense of harmony. In spite of the intensity of the psychic forces, I continued to sink deeper and deeper into this peace. Coming out of meditation, I am once again overwhelmed with gratitude.

March 24

Today my guide began by doing some healing and balancing on all my subtle bodies and chakras. She then prompted me to visualize myself as Vajradhara. As I did this, I felt his clarity permeating all levels of myself. My etheric body seemed electric. My astral body was infused with enthusiasm and warmth. My mental body was sparkling like a star. She then told me to meditate on Vajradhara, which aroused some strong negative feelings in me. The youthful optimism and positiveness of Vajradhara challenged my resistance to being here on earth. I have found it very difficult to embrace the psychic and material pollution of our world. I have a very low tolerance for the greed, violence, and exploitation that oppresses the globe. I had a clear insight today; if I could stay focused in the Vajradhara state of awareness I would be unaffected by these environmental forces. In fact, this would also be the most beneficial thing I could do for the rest of the world. Vajradhara is "the holder of the vajra," the power of the indestructible Void. By remaining in the Vajradhara state of consciousness, and not succumbing to the constant flux of feeling judgments and negative thoughts, I could be a receiving and sending unit for the Vajradhara vibration in this dimension.

March 25

My guide began today's session by aligning and clearing my chakras and subtle bodies. She then sat in front of me in deep meditation and projected the image of Vajradhara into my sixth chakra. I meditated on this image for the entire session. I realized that if all my actions would stem from this level, my life would be automatically directed by the creative power of the cosmos. While I meditated on Vajradhara, I felt that my mental body was being programmed to function from his perspective.

March 26

My guide came and sat in front of me and went into a deep meditation. There was light radiating from her, and I went into resonance with it. This took me immediately into the Void.

During this last month I have been having special dreams. At the end of meditation today, I remembered a dream I had last night in which there was a flow of energy coming out of my hands as I entered a new dimension of consciousness. Recalling the experience of the dream, I found myself transported to a past life. I was a hermit sitting in a cave in India absorbed in meditation. As I went deeper into that life, I saw that my life was lived in serenity and harmony with nature.

In juxtaposition to the serenity I experienced today, I am acutely aware of the anxiety and tension that I carry in my present body. I saw today how wonderful it would be to live without them.

March 27

This morning my guide dissolved into the Void shortly after she sat in front of me to meditate. I was left to contemplate the emptiness that we exist in. I sank deeper and deeper into this emptiness until I felt like I was at the bottom of the ocean again. No matter how tumultuous the surface of life is, the depths of the Void are always calm. I am getting a clearer idea of what life could be like lived from the depths of this "calm abiding."

March 28

Today my guide assumed the yabyum position and raised the Kundalini force once again. As I became aware of the pressure in my sixth chakra, I remembered a dream from the night before. In the dream, Kundalini had risen up the central channel and pierced open the petals of the sixth chakra to reveal a jewel that sparkled with a diamond light. I felt that some great secret had been revealed to me—the meaning of the mantra OM MANI PADME

Figure 37. Vajrapani is depicted in Tantric iconography as a blue
Bodhisattva surrounded by flames, symbolizing the wisdom that
destroys all obstacles. He wields a dorje and another rests on top of his
crown. He also wears the jewelry of a Bodhisattva and a serpent belt.
His powerful form steps to the right on a seed pod of a lotus blossom.
The blossom and seeds of the lotus develop at that same time. This is
a Tantric symbol for both the unity in multiplicity, and the synchronous
relationship of cause and effect. Contemporary painting by Äge
Delbanco reproduced by permission of the artist.

HUM. I kept trying to tell people this in my dream because I was afraid that I might forget this insight.

Near the end of the session, I had a spontaneous image of the door of a blazing furnace being opened and the fire of Kundalini burned in me like a raging fire. As the flames gradually subsided, a peace descended upon me. Again feelings of gratitude welled up from within.

March 29

At the beginning of the session, I was struck with an aura of ceremony. As I focused my attention on the inner planes, I became aware of about a hundred Tibetan monks. They were chanting, and it seemed like the atmosphere was filled with incense. And suddenly I found myself reliving a dream from the night before. I was walking onto a platform that was painted to look like it wasn't there. I was afraid to step onto it, but was impelled to. Next, I noticed a high voltage electrical wire running across the platform. I couldn't see very well and was afraid of trying to step over it because I didn't want to be electrocuted. I was then watching myself in the dream. I looked like an angelic being wearing a long white robe. When I stepped across the wire, I passed into another dimension and my field of vision appeared as if I was looking through a kaleidoscope. Being in all these places at once confused me, I didn't know where I was. My normal concepts of space and time were useless. Looking "down," I saw an image moving toward me. When it got closer, I saw it was a Tibetan deity. I had an uncanny feeling that I had seen it before, yet I didn't recognize it. I remember trying to hold the image of the deity before me, but it finally faded away.

In meditation the same deity reappeared. As the monks continued to chant, my guide told me to contemplate this deity. I was most impressed with the power of this deity, he seemed to embody the power of Tantra. His body was consumed in a spiral of flames and he was dynamically stepping out on his right leg. I felt his fire burning in me, it was a transformational energy. The chanting of the monks intensified. I began to get the idea that I was going through an initiation. I kept getting the impression that it had something to do with teaching, that I was being empowered to teach Tantra. I mistrusted these thoughts, I suspected my ego was being tempted again. I later discovered that this deity was Vajrapani. One of the implications of the Vajrapani initiation is the potential to spread the seeds of realization as realization blossoms within us.

◇

Seven years later, as I complete this manuscript, I'm still remaining mindful, watching for the seeds of these inner experiences to blossom in my outer life. Looking back, it seems that the intensity of the inner fire purged me to my very core. After six months of the most incredible "peak experience," the dross began spewing out into my external life. These last seven years have been one intense drama after another, the deepest and darkest karmic patterns within me have been relentlessly quickened by the power of Kundalini.

Though the snares of karma and ego still strain to hold me, the freedom that the Tantric path leads to becomes more apparent each day. My conviction and knowingness grow while my pride and defensiveness are worn away, yet I still wonder from time to time, will the necessity for letting go ever cease? But I know it won't, the Tantric path is endless; there is no place to be, no where to come from, no one to be, and no-thing to become. This is the essence of the Wisdom Gone Beyond.

Glossary of
Jungian Terms

Anima: the feminine side of a man's psyche

Animus: the masculine side of a woman's psyche

Archetype: images or psychic configurations in the collective depths of the psyche defining the parameters of the personal identity.

Collective Unconscious: the sum total of unconscious transpersonal elements of the psyche.

Individuation: a gradual expansion of the boundaries of the personal identity leading to an integration of increasing amounts of repressed personal and transpersonal factors. A sense of wholeness and completeness are thereby attained.

Self: The complete sphere of archetypal and transpersonal factors of the psyche acting as a unifying or transcendental force.

Shadow: the socially unacceptable and personally rejected aspects of the psyche that may act as autonomous subpersonalities below the normal level of awareness of the ego-self.

◇

Glossary of
Tantric Terms

Abhidharma: a metaphysical and philosophical branch of the Buddhist doctrine.

Arhat: literally "the victorious one," a term used in Hinayana Buddhism to refer to the practitioner who leaves the wheel of birth and death by entering nirvana.

Bardo: literally "an in-between state" usually applied to the period between death and rebirth.

Bija-Mantra: a seed syllable denoting a specific cosmic or psychic force, used in mantras and visualizations.

Bindu (Thig-Le in Tibetan): literally "point," denoting potent points of emptiness or seed-essence.

Bodhicitta: "Enlightened Mind-Heart" of a Buddha. Metaphorically visualized as a milk-white bliss-creating nectar, and generally related to as a compassionate attitude and motivation to reach enlightenment for the benefit of all sentient beings.

Bodhisattva: a person who strives to generate Bodhicitta and vows a life of selfless service, including renouncing nirvana until all beings reach enlightenment.

Buddha: either the person Gautama, founder of Buddhism, or any awakened being.

Chakra: "wheel" used to describe the major psychic energy centers along the spine.

Dakini: "sky-goer," a female spirit who imparts secret knowledge.

Dharma: the combined teachings of Gautama Buddha, or universal law.

Dharmakaya: the supernal body of the Buddha-Mind.

Gelupa: one of the major sects of Tibetan Buddhism

Guru: "Bringer of Light," *i.e.*, a teacher.

Heruka: any wrathful expression of the Buddha-Mind used as a deity in higher Tantric practices.

Hinayana: "The Lesser Vehicle," the original form of Buddhism propagated by Gautama Buddha's students.

Ida: the feminine secondary psychic channel along the spine.

Jina: conqueror, the name given to the five primordial Buddhas because their wisdom dispells the illusions of the ego-mind.

Jnana: the cognitive state innate in the Void, and thus the quintessence of Wisdom.

Kargyu: one of the major sects of Tibetan Buddhism

Karma: literally "action," referring to the cause and effect relationship between our mental, emotional, and physical actions and their results in our lives.

Klesa: a karmic obscuration caused by desire or delusion that functions as an obstacle on the path to enlightenment.

Lama: a Tibetan Buddhist monk or teacher highly educated in Buddhist, and/or Tantric, doctrines and practice.

Madhyamika: a school of philosophy that served as the precursor to the expanded doctrine of Mahayana Buddhism, based on the theory of Voidness, and initiated by the sage Nagarjuna in the second century A.D.

Mahamudra: literally, "the great gesture." The Great Seal or symbol pointing toward the highest attainment of the Tantric path, the union of perfect insight into Voidness and Liberation.

Mahayana: "The Great Vehicle," in juxtaposition to the Hinayana, or "Lesser Vehicle." An expanded doctrine distinct in that it is based on the Bodhisattva Vow, a large pantheon of deities, meditation on the Void, and the importance of the guru over the word of scripture.

Mandala: the divine circle used in meditation representing particular psychic or cosmic forces. Jung considered mandalas to be an expression of the Self, the healing or whole-making aspect of the psyche.

Mantra: a sacred chant that produces certain psychic effects. Each deity has its own mantra, used to invoke its qualities in meditation.

Maya: the great apparition of the phenomenal world, associated with the feminine power of creation in Hindu Tantra.

Mudra: a gesture that symbolizes the quality of a particular deity.

Nada: a subtle pathway of psychic energy in the body-mind.

Nirmanakaya: an incarnate Buddha

Nirvana: "to extinguish or expire," the liberation from the suffering caused by delusions of the ego-self.

Nyingmapa: a major sect of Tibetan Buddhism

Pingala: the masculine secondary channel of psychic energy along the spine.

Prana: the psychic energy associated with the breath, related to different chakras and states of mind, that circulates through the subtle pathways of the body-mind.

Prajna: heightened awareness, associated with female deities in Buddhist Tantra.

Samadhi: literally "union with the Lord," a profound state of meditation in which the Void nature of reality is realized, synonymous with enlightenment.

Sambogakaya: the astral or illusionary body of the Buddha-Mind. The form that the meditational deities appear in during meditation or dream yoga.

Samsara: a state of cyclic existence conditioned by the ignorance and suffering of the ego-self.

Siddhi: an attainment of powers or skills, either mundane or spiritual.

Shunyata: "emptiness." In Tantric usage it denotes the Void nature of reality.

Sushumna: the primary or central psychic channel along the spine in which Kundalini arises.

Tantra: an ancient verb "to weave," implying the continuous interwoven-ness of male and female cosmic forces creating the fabric of reality. As a body of teaching, it employs a pantheon of deities and their specific meditation rituals.

Tathata: the "suchness" or precise elements composing any phenomena; on another level, the principal attributes of existence, *i.e.*, the Void

Thig-Le: see *Bindu*

Tulku: a recognized reincarnation of an enlightened being, theoretically an emanation of the Buddha-Mind.

Vajra: adamantine or indestructible and pristine, like a diamond, used to symbolize the Void.

Vajrayana: the Tantric school of Mahayana Buddhism.

Yabyum: literally "Father-Mother," referring to the male and female deities in Tantric sexual embrace and symbolizing the union of Wisdom and Compassion.

Yantra: a symbolic diagram that invokes a specific deity.

Yidam: any male or female deity used as an object of meditation.

Yoga: literally, "yoke," implying the union of the mundane and sublime within the body-mind. In general, it includes various physical and mental methods employed to encourage this union.

◇

Bibliography

Anderson, Walt. *Open Secrets.* New York: Penguin, 1979.

Bailey, Alice. *Esoteric Healing.* New York: Lucis Publishing Co., 1977.

Bentove, Itzhak. "Micromotion of the Body as a Factor in the Development of the Nervous System," in *Kundalini Evolution and Enlightenment.* (John White, ed.) New York: Doubleday, Anchor Press, 1979.

Bernbaum, Edwin. *The Way to Shambhala.* New York: Doubleday, Anchor Press, 1980.

Blofeld, John. *Mantras, Sacred Words of Power.* London: Unwin Hyman, 1977.

———. *Tantric Mysticism of Tibet.* New York: Dutton, 1970.

Brennan, Barbara Ann. *Hands of Light.* New York: Bantam, 1987.

Campbell, Joseph. *The Mythic Image.* Bollingen Series. Princeton, NJ: Princeton University Press, 1974.

Castillejo, Irene Claremont de. *Knowing Woman.* New York: Harper & Row, 1973.

Chang, Garma C. C. *The Six Yogas of Naropa and Teachings on Mahamudra.* Ithaca, NY: Snow Lion, 1963.

———. *Teachings of Tibetan Yoga.* Secaucus, NJ: Citadel Press, 1963.

Cozort, David. *Highest Yoga Tantra*. Ithaca, NY: Snow Lion, 1986.

Curtis, Helena. *Biology*. NY: Worth Publishers, 1968.

Devananda, Swami Vishnu. *Meditation and Mantras*. Somewhere, NY: Om Lotus, 1978.

Dorje, Wang Chug, The Ninth Karmapa. *The Mahamudra*. Dharamsala, India: Library of Tibetan Works and Archives, 1978.

Douglas, Nik, and Penny Slinger. *Sexual Secrets*. Rochester, VT: Destiny Books, 1979.

Dowman, Keith. *Masters of Mahamudra*. Albany, NY: State University of New York Press, 1985.

Evans-Wentz, W. Y. *The Tibetan Book of the Dead*. New York: Oxford University Press, 1960.

———. *Tibetan Yoga and Secret Doctrines*. London and New York: Oxford University Press, 1958.

Gawain, Shakti. *Creative Visualization*. Mill Valley, CA: Whatever Publishing, 1978.

Govinda, Lama. *Creative Meditation and Multi-Dimensional Consciousness*. Wheaton, IL: Theosophical Publishing House, 1976.

———. *Foundations of Tibetan Mysticism*. York Beach, ME: Samuel Weiser, 1974; and London: Rider & Co., 1974.

The Hundred Thousand Songs of Milarepa.

Jaffe, Aniela. *The Myth of Meaning*. New York: Penguin Books, 1975.

Jung, Carl. *Aion*. Bollingen Series. Princeton, NJ: Princeton University Press, 1959.

———. *Analytical Psychology: Its Theory and Practice*. New York: Vintage Books, 1968.

———. *Aspects of the Feminine*. Bollingen Series. Princeton, NJ: Princeton University Press, 1982.

————. Aniela Jaffe, ed. "Septem Sermones ad Mortuos," in *Memories, Dreams, Reflections*. New York: Random House, 1965.

————. *The Psychology of the Transference*. Princeton, NJ: Princeton University Press, 1966.

Khanna, Madhu. *Yantra*. London: Thames and Hudson, 1979.

Kongtrul, Jamgon. *The Torch of Certainty*. Boston: Shambhala, 1986.

Kornfield, Jack. *Living Buddhist Masters*. Santa Cruz, CA: Unity Press, 1977.

La Berge, Stephen. *Lucid Dreaming*. New York: Ballantine, 1985.

Leonard, George. *The Silent Pulse*. New York: Dutton, 1978.

The Life of Teresa of Jesus. Quoted in *The Laughing Man*, Vol. 2, No. 2. San Rafael, CA: Dawn Horse Press, 1981, p. 50.

Longchenpa. Herbert Guenther, tr. "Wonderment," from *Kindly Bent to Ease*. Berkeley, CA: Dharma Press, 1976.

Miller, Emmett, M.D., *Software for the Mind*. Berkeley, CA: Celestial Arts, 1987.

Moacanin, Radmila. *Jung's Psychology and Tibetan Buddhism*. Newburyport, MA and London: Wisdom Publications, 1986.

Monroe, Robert A. *Journeys Out of the Body*. New York: Doubleday, 1971.

Muses, Charles. *The Esoteric Teachings of the Tibetan Tantra*. York Beach, ME: Samuel Weiser, 1961.

Neumann, Erich. *The Origins and History of Consciousness*. Bollingen Series. Princeton, NJ: Princeton University Press, 1954.

Pachem Lama, The First. *The Great Seal of Voidness*. Dharamsala, India: Library of Tibetan Works and Archives, 1975.

Powell, Robert. *The Blissful Life*. Durham, NC: The Acorn Press, 1984.

Ramsdale, David Alan, and Ellen Jo Dorfman. *Sexual Energy Ecstasy*. Playa Del Ray, CA: Peak Skill Publishing, 1985.

Rawson, Philip. *Tantra: The Indian Cult of Ecstasy*. New York: Avon, 1973.

Ray, R. Nancy Falk and Rita Gross, eds. "Accomplished Women in Tantric Buddhism," in *Unspoken Worlds*. New York: Harper & Row, 1980.

Roberts, Jane. *The Nature of the Psyche*. New York: Prentice Hall, 1979.

Rudhyar, Dane. *Occult Preparations for a New Age*. Wheaton, IL: Theosophical Publishing, 1975.

Sanford, John A. *Healing and Wholeness*. New York: Paulist Press, 1977.

Sangpo, Khetsun, Rinbochay. *Tantric Practice in Nying-Mapa*. New York: Snow Lion, 1982.

Sole-Leris, Amadeo. *Tranquility and Insight*. Boston: Shambhala, 1986.

Stevens, Dr. Ian. *Twenty Cases of Suggestive Reincarnation*. Charlottesville, VA: University Press of Virginia, 1974.

Thompson, William Irwin. *Passages About Earth*. New York: Harper & Row, 1974.

Trungpa, Chogyam. *Cutting Through Spiritual Materialism*. Boston: Shambhala, 1973.

Tulku, Tarthang. *Openness Mind*. Berkeley, CA: Dharma Publishing, 1978.

Walle, J. H., and Nanta & Michael Feirtag. "The Organization of the Brain." *Scientific American*. September 1979, Vol. 241, p. 97.

Willson, Martin. *Rebirth and the Western Buddhist*. Newburyport, MA and London: Wisdom Publications, 1987.

Yakswaranda, Swami. "A Glimpse into the Hindu Religious Symbology," in *Cultural Heritage of India*. Edited by Sri Rama Krishna Centenary Committee. Calcutta, India: Belur Math. Vol. 2,

Yeshe, Lama Thubten. *Wisdom Energy*. Honolulu: The Conch Press, 1976.

INDEX